1 Handful of kale
2 Handful spinach
6 Stalks celery
3 Spray of parsley
1 Lemons
1 Limes
Bulb fennel
1 Beet
3 Carrot

6 Carrots
1 Beet
1 Cucumber

- 1 Beet
- Carrots
- 1 Cup Strawberries
- 6-8 Kale leaves
- 3 Cucumbers

2 Beets
6 Carrots
2 Stalks of Celery
Lemon

9 Carrots
Spinach or Lettuce
Kale
Lemon

9 Carrots
2 Cucumbers
2 Oranges
Ginger

Spinach or Kale
Celery
3 Cucumbers
8 Carrots
2 Green Apples
2 Oranges
Ginger

Grapefruit
Lemon
Oranges
Pineapple

2 Carrot
1 Apple
6 Celery Ribs
1 Beet
Parsley or Cilantro
Ginger

Apples
Celery
Ginger
Lemon
Orange
Spinach

Celery
Cucumber
Orange
Parsley
Ginger
Lemon

1 Handful of Kale or Spinach
2 Cucumbers
1 Granny Smith Apple
Lime
Ginger

1 apple
1 lemon
1 piece fresh gingerroot
ice
filtered water

1/2 cups rice milk
1/2 cups silken tofu
1/3 cups creamy peanut butter
2 fresh bananas

2 cups brewed double strength coffee
1 pint coffee ice cream
6 cups ice
1 1/2 cups skim milk
Whipped cream (optional)
Cinnamon/Chocolate

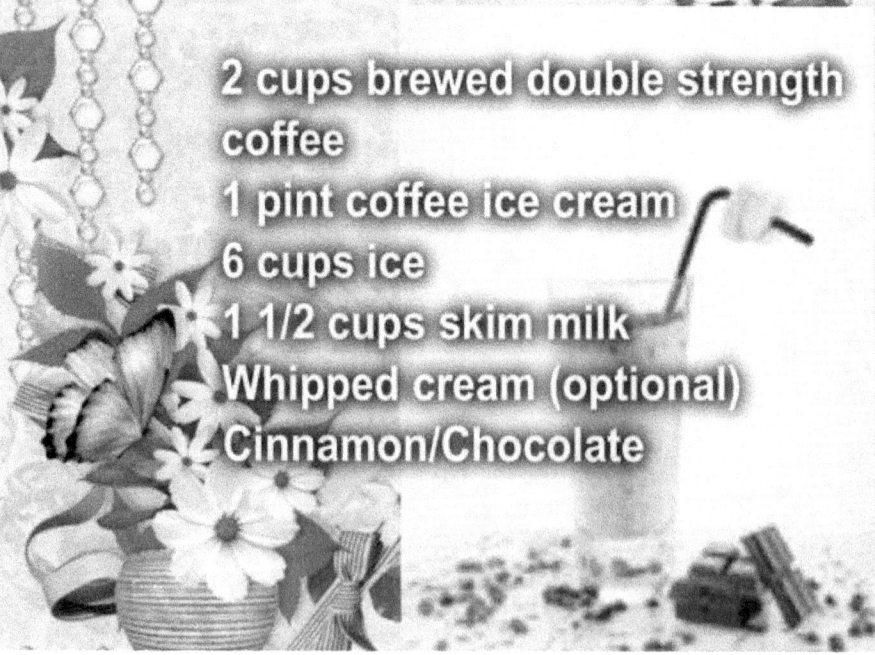

1/2 cups plain or vanilla yogurt
1 1/2 cups frozen blackberries
1 banana
1/2 bag of frozen blueberries
2 tablespoons blueberry preserves
7 or 8 ice cubes
1 1/2 cups of soymilk

- 3 small ice cubes
- 2 apricots
- 1/2 papaya
- 1/2 mango
- 1/2 cups carrot juice
- 1 tablespoon honey

4 medium bananas
light brown sugar
hazelnuts
1/4 cups milk
1/4 cups dark rum
or hazelnut liqueur
banana liqueur
vanilla syrup
half and half
ice cubes
chopped walnuts

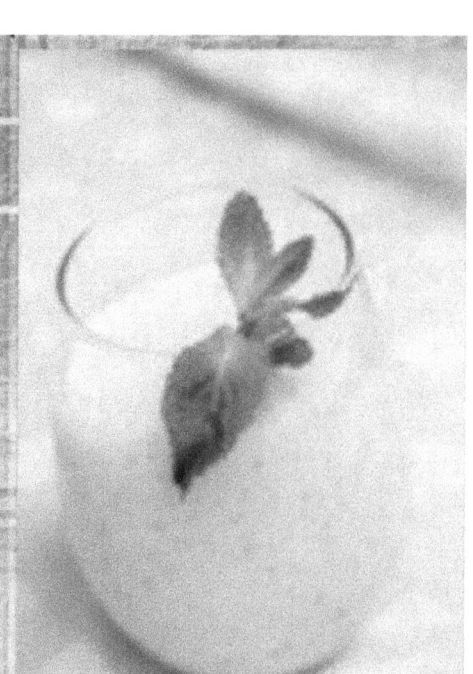

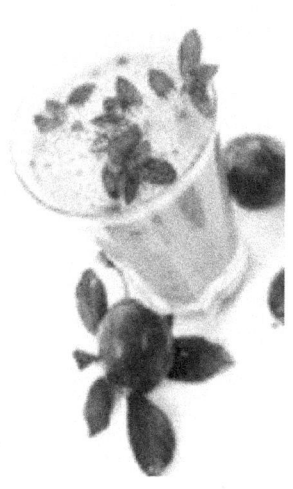

1 large avocado
2 teaspoons condensed milk
1 cup ice
frozen bananas
4 to 5 strawberries
nonfat soy/nut milk
cardamom
allspice

1 peach, frozen
10 blueberries
1 cup light vanilla yogurt
milk
crushed pecan
teaspoons salt
teaspoons vanilla extract

kefir
half a cup of non-fat milk
a frozen banana
peanut butter
some almonds

1 cup blueberry yogurt
2 cups frozen blueberries
1 scoop vanilla whey protein powder
1 scoop blueberry flavoured VegeGreens

5 or 6 frozen banana slices
1 cup frozen fruit
cup vanilla yoghurt
cup milk
1 teaspoon Splenda

cucumbers
kale
fresh mint
fresh parsley
fresh ginger
1 avocado
1 cup coconut water
juice of 1 lime
udo's, hemp or flaxseed oil
hemp seeds or chia seeds
liquid stevia

1 banana, sliced
1 cup mixed frozen berries (raspberries, blueberries, strawberries)
1 cup milk of your choice

1 cup broccoli florets
1/4 of an avocado
1 banana
1 peach
1 cup unsweetened almond milk
1/4 cup ice cubes

cooked navy beans
frozen mango or papaya
soy milk
honey

1 cup frozen strawberries
1/4 cup ricotta
milk
honey

My Favorite Quote About The Smoothie Lifestyle

While every precaution has been taken in the preparation of this book, the publisher assumes no responsibility for errors or omissions, or for damages resulting from the use of the information contained herein.

BLENDER COOKBOOK: 60 BLENDER COCKTAILS RECIPES FOR BODY CLEANSE & DETOX, ENERGY, VITALITY & RAPID WEIGHT LOSS

First edition. July 11, 2017.

Copyright © 2017 Juliana Baltimoore.

Written by Juliana Baltimoore.

Why Drinking Smoothies Is Important

You should read this book because in this book you will find superfoods that are very beneficial for your health and they will keep your body lean and clean.

Taking in all these superfoods via smoothies on a daily basis is going to benefit you because you are going to keep your body disease free and best of all drinking these smoothies on a daily basis is keeping the doctor far far away!

These are the 18 secret superfoods and what they can do for your body and mind.

1. Avocado

Avocados contain anti cancer benefits

Avocados do promotes the health of your heart

Avocados do support your cardiovascular health

Sufficient amounts of oleic acid also do improve your cardiovascular system

Potassium is important because it regulates your blood pressure

Avocados have a wide range of anti inflammatory benefits

Avocados do promote the blood sugar regulation

Avocados have 18 amino acids that are required to form complete protein that is used more efficiently by your body than proteins that are found in meat foods

Avocados are high in fiber contents and they aid in digestion and total body absorption of nutrients

Avocados do contain more natural fiber than any other fruit

The Healthy fats found in avocados raises the "good" cholesterol while lowering the "bad" cholesterol and the triglycerides by 20%

Avocados also contain 35% more potassium than bananas do

Avocados do provide the lutein that is necessary to protect you from age related eye degeneration problems

The anti inflammatory properties of avocado fruits do prevent and treat rheumatoid arthritis

Oleic acid helps protect you against prostate and breast cancer

It also helps keep your nervous system healthy & fit

Avocados have shown to increase collagen production of the skin as well as reduce the size and appearance of wrinkles

Avocados are considered one of the nature's most effective moisturizers for the skin

Glutathione that is contained in avocados boosts your immune system

Avocado Beauty Tips:

Mix the pulp of an avocado and apply it as a masque directly to your face and body skin

If you suffer from sunburn, eczema, dry spots or psoriasis, the healthy fat in avocado protects, repairs and moisturizes your skin

The pulp closest to the avocado skin has the highest concentration of nutrients

Make sure to use this pulp and scrape it off the skin

Apply this pulp directly to the skin for a soft and a supple result

2. Blueberries

These are the benefits of blueberries:

Whole body antioxidant support

Cardiovascular benefits

Cognitive benefits

Blood sugar benefits

Eye health

Anti cancer benefits

3. Coconut

These are the benefits of coconut:

Coconuts do helps prevent obesity

Coconut improves your heart health

Coconut is high in dietary fiber and contains a low glycemic index

Coconut helps reduces sweet cravings and improves your digestion

Coconut gives a quick boost of energy

In addition, coconut contains no trans fats

Coconut is gluten free, non toxic and hypoallergenic

It also contains antiviral, antibacterial, antifungal, and anti parasitic healing properties for the body

Coconut helps your overall immune system functions

4. Ginger

These are the benefits of ginger:

Gastrointestinal relief

Safe and effective relief of nausea

anti inflammatory effects

Protection against colorectal cancer

Ginger induces cell death in ovarian cancer cells

Immune boosting action

5. Kale

These are the benefits of kale:

Antioxidant related health benefits

Anti inflammatory health benefits

Glucosinolates and cancer preventive benefits

Glucosinolates in kale and their detox activating isothiocyanates

Cardiovascular support

Other health related benefits

6. Rasperries

These are the benefits of rasperries:

Antioxidant and anti inflammatory benefits

Obesity and blood sugar benefits

Anti cancer benefits

7. Papaya

These are the benefits of papaya:

Protection against heart disease

Anti inflammatory effects

Promotes digestive health

Immune support

Protection against rheumatoid arthritis
Papaya and green tea in combination prevents prostate cancer

8. Broccoli
These are the benefits of broccoli:
The cancer-inflammation-oxidative stress-detox connection
anti Inflammatory benefits
antioxidant benefits
broccoli can enhance detoxification
broccoli and cancer prevention
broccoli and digestive support
broccoli and cardiovascular support

9. Apricot
These are the benefits of apricot:
Apricots do protect your eyesight
Apricots do contain nutrients (vitamin A for good vision and it is also a powerful antioxidant, Vitamin A quenches the free radical damage to cells and tissues)

10. Banana
These are the benefits of bananas:
Cardiovascular protection from potassium and fiber
soothing protection from ulcers
improving elimination
protect your eyesight
build better bones with bananas
Bananas do promote kidney health through regular and moderate intake

11. Pecan Nuts
These are the benefits of pecan nuts:
Pecan nuts are the best antioxidants on earth
Pecan nuts do help in weight loss
Pecan nuts also help prevent coronary heart diseases
Pecan nuts contain a rich source of vitamin E (a natural antioxidant that protects the blood lipids from getting oxidized)
Pecan nuts also have cholesterol lowering properties
The plant sterols in pecans have cholesterol lowering characteristics
Pecan nuts do help increase the metabolic rate of your body

Pecan nuts do improve satiety

Pecans also contain 19 plus vitamins & minerals that your body needs

Pecans do contain vitamines from the B group, vitamine A, vitamine E, calcium, potassium, folic acid, phosphorus, zinc, magnesium, and many more

Pecan nuts are a rich source of proteins and they do contain less carbohydrates

Pecans contain zero cholesterol

Pecans are also best suited for a sodium restricted diet

Pecans are recommended to heart patients

People with high blood pressure should be eating pecans because these nuts are sodium free

12. Walnuts

Walnuts have cardiovascular benefits

Walnuts help reduce problems in metabolic syndrome

Walnuts are beneficial in treatment of type 2 diabetes

Walnuts have anti cancer benefits

Walnuts have anti inflammatory nutrients which is perfect for the support of your bone health

A large amount of walnuts decreases your blood levels of N-telopeptides of type 1 collagen

Walnuts are a desirable food for support of weight loss and for prevention of obesity

Walnuts are unique in their collection of anti inflammatory nutrients

These nutrients include omega 3 fatty acids

Walnuts also promote anti cancer benefits

13. Carrots

Carrots have a rich supply of antioxidant nutrients called beta carotene

These delicious orange vegetables are the source not only of beta carotene, but also of a wide variety of antioxidants plus other health supporting nutrients.

Other benefits of carrots:

Antioxidant benefits

Cardiovascular benefits

Vision health

14. Lemon

Lemons are very alkalizing for the body and they do help to restore the balance of the pH

Lemons are rich in flavonoids and vitamin C

Vitamin C works against infections like colds and the flu

Lemons are a wonderful stimulantion to your liver

Lemon is a dissolvent of uric acid and other poisons

It is a is a great liver detoxifier

It cleanses your bowels

Lemons increase peristalsis in the bowels

The citric acid in lemon juice helps to dissolve calcium deposits, gallstones and kidney stones

Vitamin C in lemons helps the body to neutralize free radicals that are linked to most types of diseases and aging

Lemon peel contains phytonutrient tangeretin

Phytonutrient Tangeretin has been proven to be effective for brain disorders (Parkinson disease for example)

Lemons destroy intestinal worms

In a condition of insufficient oxygen and breathing problems (mountain climbing, etc.) lemons are very helpful

Some other helpful facts about lemons:

Scurvy is treated by giving 1-2 ounces of lemon juice with water every 2 to 4 hours

Tip:

Mix the juice of one lemon or lime to warm water and drink this mixture first thing in the morning to start your day

15. Peanuts

These are the benefits of peanuts:

Peanuts are a rich source of antioxidants

Heart health benefits

Potentially reduced risk of strokes

Helps prevent gallstones

Protects against Alzheimer and other age related cognitive decline health problems

Lowers risk of weight gain

16. Cinnamon

Cinnamon contains anti clotting actions as well as anti microbial activity

Cinnamon controls the blood sugar

Cinnamon's scent helps boost your brain functions

Calcium & fiber improves the colon health & helps protect you against heart disease

Cinnamon is a traditional warming remedy and the perfect winter spice

Enjoy cinnamon with a hot lemon to fight the cold

17. Pineapple

Pineapple contains anti inflammatory & digestive benefits

Pineapple provides your body with an antioxidant protection and gives immune support

Pineapple acts as protection against macular degeneration

Vitamix Versus Nutribullet

I have always loved my Vitamix more than the Nutribullet at first because the Vitamix is just many more things that just a regular old blender.

I use my Vitamix to grind up herbs, grains, veggies, fruits, flax seeds, and whatever ingredient I like to add to my Smoothies.

As you can imagine, I was pretty sceptic when I first heard about the Nutribullet. I did not believe that any other kitchen aid might be comparable to the Vitamix because for me the Vitamix is just ninja powerful.

The Vitamix still peaked my curiosity because I just love new kitchen tools and appliances.

Since I am also a consultant myself, I am constantly looking for new trends and kitchen supplies to tell my clients about. I am constantly looking for more affordable and less expensive kitchen supplies because not everybody can afford to buy high prized kitchen stuff.

I decided to give the Nutribullet a shot and compare it to my Vitamix.

The following are my own results:

The Nutribullet ground up every ingredient that I fed into it and I was totally surprised. The first smoothie that I made with it was chunk free when I tasted it and the consistency was totally smooth.

I was totally floored with the results and decide to give it some more experimenting time.

I was able to grind up even the leafiest greens and even goji berries and to my surprise even with better results than with a standard kitchen blender.

I love how the milling blade of the Nutribullet grinds up flax seeds into flax meal and in such an effortless fashion.

Overall, I think that the Nutribullet is the perfect alternative to the Vitamix. It is truly an inexpensive alternative for the expensive and high end Vitamix blender.

It is perfect for someone who is starting out with smoothies and who is looking for an easy way to make smoothies and other blender recipes an affordable investment.

What is still surprising me to this day is that the Nutribullet is very similar to the Vitamix blender. The Nutribullet works very well for grinding grains and even nuts.

The differences between the Nutribullet and the Vitamix are really minor.

After having gone through the test, I believe that the Nutribullet is even the better option because it is just a better deal in terms of investment for what you are getting. It is in my opinion the best option for everyone who is looking for a healthy lifestyle and who does not want to invest too much money upfront in order to get started.

This test and experimenting phase has also let me to the conclusion that I want to help people who are just getting started with a Smoothie diet or with a Smoothie lifestyle.

Since I want to make a healthy diet and a healthy lifestyle achievable and affordable for real people in real life, I went ahead and created a collection of Smoothie recipes just for people who already invested in the Nutribullet or who are going to invest in the Nutribullet in the near future in order to better their life.

The upcoming collection of smoothies has been created with the Nutribullet. I created these Nutribullet recipes for real people that have one goal in mind: Getting started with a realistic healthy diet and a healthy lifestyle like the smoothie diet because they know it is achievable and the Nutribullet is going to help them make their choice an affordable choice.

Let's get started with the scrumptious & healthy smoothie recipes that you can quickly and easily make with your own Nutribullet, too!

Scrumptious & Healthy Pound Dropping Smoothies

Unlike juices, fruit and veggie smoothies also retain all fibers (whole raw fruits & veggies). It is important to eat fiber on a daily basis and fiber is one of the least expensive ways to prevent illnesses.

Fibers do helps the body eliminate toxins and wasted stuff.

Smoothies supply the body with an unlimited amount of health benefits like:

* Elimination & digestion gets improved
* Weight loss
* Substitution for soft drinks & snacks:
* Satisfying Meal replacement

Lots More as you will soon discover for yourself...

Quick n'Easy 5 Minute Easy Peach Pistachio Smoothie

Ingredients:

1 small organic and chopped banana

1 small juicy pitted peach, organic if possible

½ cup of organic pistachios, make sure to buy them finely chopped or chop them yourself

¼ cup of pure and organic coconut milk

Directions:

Mix all the above organic ingredients in your favorite blender (we recommend the Nutribullet) until everything is deliciously smooth

Creamy Strawberry Smoothie

"Show Me The Smoothies!" Famous Smoothie Quote

If you love tasty smoothies with some strange secret ingredients that are heavenly deliciously then you might consider the Strawberry n'Creams smoothie.

Imagine the best of creams and cheeses combined with some zesty red fruits like strawberries or rasperries.

Pouring the contents of a delightful fruit-cream-cheese platter into your favorite blender (in my case I am using the Vitamix) and whip it all together into a creamy delight.

This cheese, cream and strawberry smoothie drink contains the following ingredients:

Ingredients:
    1 cup frozen rasperries or strawberries whatever you prefer or have available
    1/4 cup of fresh organic Italian ricotta cheese

1/2 cup of milk or skim milk (depending on your goals and if you are on a diet just use the skim milk and do not add the rich cream)

A Dash of rich tasty cream to swirl this into a creamy and rich tasting delight

Raw organic Honey (optional and to your taste)

Directions:

For all these Smoothie recipe simply follow my 5 Minute Easy n'Quick Smoothie Preparation Power Tips To Maximize Your Pound Dropping Results in the section below.

Add all the ingredients into your Vitamix or similar high-speed blender. Make sure to add fresh spring water. Add as much water as you like in order to reach your desired thickness of the smoothie. For all the smoothie recipes, make sure to use organic products, fruits and vegetables if possible.

Mix the strawberries, the ricotta cheese, the milk and the cream in a blender and swirl it into a creamy texture while adding the raw honey.

In the summer adding some additional ice cupbes might be a very very refreshing idea. Instead of the ice cubes you can also add some strawberry or rasperry sherbert or ice cream. This is totally optional and depends on your goal. If your goal is to loose weight then just skip the creamy stuff!

Enjoy this refreshing and delicious smoothie!

Quick n'Scrumptious Cinnamon Apricot Smoothie

Ingredients:
- 3 pitted and already chopped organic Apricots
- 1 pitted and already chopped organic peach
- a healthy pinch of of organic cinnamon spice
- 1 teaspoon of organic and pure maple syrup
- ice cubes to your liking

Directions:

Mix all the above organic ingredients in your favorite blender (we recommend the Nutribullet) until everything is deliciously smooth

Boost Your Body With Papaya & Mango Smoothie

"Next Time, Indiana Jones, it will Take More Than Smoothies to Save You." Famous Smoothie Quote

A combination of healthy and lean making protein and mango is what this smoothie is all about. The Mango Protein booster is perfect if your goal is to follow a lean and clean smoothie diet.

So what is the secret of this protein booster?

Usually smoothies are well known for their high protein content because they do rely on protein powder.

The secret ingredient fot the Mango Protein booster however is the protein of the cooked navy beans.

You might not like the idea of combining beans into your smoothies, but I am going to change your paradim quickly after you had your first serving.

I have tested this smoothie with a lot of smoothie lovers before adding it to my collection. I am constantly testing and proving new smoothie recipes that I am gradually adding to my "Tested & Proven Smoothie Recipe Collection"

This one has passed the test because it is not only delicious, but it is such a health treat and perfect for you if you are trying to loose weight with smoothies.

Between the navy beans and the soy milk that is included in this smoothie, you are going to consume around ten to eleven grams of pure protein.

This protein rich smoothie drink contains the following ingredients:

Ingredients:

1/3 cup of cooked navy beans (organic if possible)

1-1/2 cups of frozen papaya or mango

3/4 cups of organic soy milk

2 teaspoons of raw honey (this is optional and try organic raw honey if you can)

Directions:

For all these Smoothie recipe simply follow my 5 Minute Easy n'Quick Smoothie Preparation Power Tips To Maximize Your Pound Dropping Results in the section below.

Add all the ingredients into your Vitamix or similar high-speed blender. Make sure to add fresh spring water if needed. Add as much water as you like in order to reach your desired thickness of the smoothie.

For all the smoothie recipes, make sure to use organic products, fruits and vegetables if possible.

Mix the cooked navy beans and the tropical frozen fruits (mango or papaya) together and process them in your high speed blender until both ingredients are well combined together. Next, add the organic soy milk and the raw honey and continue mixing until everything is combined into a nice and creamy texture. Add ice if needed and to your own liking.

You can adjust the raw organic honey to your preference or you can skip this step if you do not have a sweet tooth or if you are following a strict smoothie diet with unsweatened smoothies.

Pumpkin Smoothie

Ingredients:

3/4 cups pure and pureed pumpkin (farm fresh or bought in a health or specialty store)

1/3 cup of full fat coconut milk

1/4 cup of fresh source water

1/2 cup of ice

2 teaspoon of pure honey

2 teaspoon of organic cinnamon spice

1/2 teaspoon of nutmeg spice

1/2 teaspoon of pumpkin pie spice

Directions:

For all these Smoothie recipe simply follow my 5 Minute Easy n'Quick Smoothie Preparation Power Tips To Maximize Your Pound Dropping Results in the section below.

Add all the ingredients into your Vitamix or similar high-speed blender. Make sure to add fresh spring water if needed. Add as much water as you like in order to reach your desired thickness of the smoothie.

For all the smoothie recipes, make sure to use organic products, fruits and vegetables if possible.

Blend all the above ingredients until smooth.

Add ice if needed and to your own liking.

You can adjust the raw organic honey to your preference or you can skip this step if you do not have a sweet tooth or if you are following a strict smoothie diet with unsweatened smoothies.

Superfood Leafy Green Shake

"Round up the Usual Fruits and Vegetables."

A fortified and nutritious combination of healthy and lean making superfood greens like broccoli and avocado.

This lean Superfood Greens Shake gets its rich flavour from the nutty tasting avocado.

Who says that vegetables are for lunch and dinner only? This lean green cocktail contains delicious and zesty fruits that are swirled into the greens and this smoothie makes for a perfect wholesome and healthy start of your day so that you do not need to wait for lunchtime to eat these healthy veggies.

This Superfood Greens Shake contains the following ingredients:

Ingredients:
1/4 of an organic avocado
1 cup of organic broccoli florets
1 peeled and organic banana that is already chopped and frozen

1 organic chopped peach or apricot or nectarine
1 cup of unsweetened and organic almond milk
ice cubes to your liking

Directions:

For all these Smoothie recipe simply follow my 5 Minute Easy n'Quick Smoothie Preparation Power Tips To Maximize Your Pound Dropping Results in the section below.

Add all the ingredients into your Vitamix or similar high-speed blender. Make sure to add fresh spring water or ice cubes if needed. Add as much water as you like in order to reach your desired thickness of the smoothie. For all the smoothie recipes, make sure to use organic products, fruits and vegetables if possible.

Mix all the ingredients together and process them with your favorite blender until all of the ingredients are well combined together. Make sure the broccoli is broken down and all the other ingredients are well swirled together in a rich looking creamy texture.

You can add more organic almond milk, water, or ice cubes (depending on your goal) if you like a more fluid and water downed smoothie. If you like you can also add some raw honey or if you are on a smoothie diet and like it sweet you can add a little bit of your favourite sweetener.

Other people love the unsweatened taste!

Quick n'5 Minute Easy Double Green Smoothie

Ingredients:
 2 organic, peeled and already chopped kiwis
 1 organic peeled, chopped and seeded orange
 ½ teaspoon of organic raw honey
 ½ cup of fresh brewed and chilled green tea (organic if possible)

Directions:

Mix all the above organic ingredients in your favorite blender (we recommend the Nutribullet) until everything is deliciously smooth

Rich Tropical Berry Screamer

1 banana, sliced
1 cup mixed frozen berries (raspberries, blueberries, strawberries)
1 cup milk of your choice

"Are you Telling Me you Built a Time Machine... out of a Vita-Mix?"

This is a refreshing blend of red, blue and black berries with or without a tropical twist.

It is a great hydration solution and thirst quencher after a physical workout.

The Rich Berry Screamer Smoothie contains the following ingredients:
Ingredients:
1 small organic banana (sliced)
1 cup of mixed frozen berries (raspberries, blueberries, blackberries, strawberries)
1 cup milk of your choice (skim if you are on a smoothie diet)
Tropical orange twist:

Nothing welcomes warmer weather better than the twist of a tropical inspired flavor from pineapples and citrus fruits like oranges and limes.

fresh orange juice

twist of lime or lemon

fresh pinapple juice

Directions:

For all these Smoothie recipe simply follow my 5 Minute Easy n'Quick Smoothie Preparation Power Tips To Maximize Your Pound Dropping Results in the section below.

Add all the ingredients into your Vitamix or similar high-speed blender. Make sure to add fresh spring water or ice cubes if needed. Add as much water as you like in order to reach your desired thickness of the smoothie. For all the smoothie recipes, make sure to use organic products, fruits and vegetables if possible.

Mix all the ingredients together and process them with your favorite blender until all of the ingredients are well combined together. Add a little filtered spring water or ice cubes if needed for your desired consistency.

Add all the ingredients to your blender and puree the mixture until everything is smooth.

Tastes Like Cake Batter Smoothie

This recipe is a delicious dessert smoothie which has the consistency similar to a milkshake along with the incredible flavor of cake batter. This smoothie is not only paleo but also gluten free and vegan.

Ingredients:
Macadamia nuts - 1 table spoon
Coconut butter (if not available coconut oil can also be used) - 1 table spoon
Banana - 1 (frozen)
Dried fig - 1 (If not available 2 dates can also be used)
Almond milk - 1 cup
Vanilla extract - 1/2 tea spoon
Raw honey and a little amount of dark chocolate chips for garnishing

Directions:
For all these Smoothie recipe simply follow my 5 Minute Easy n'Quick Smoothie Preparation Power Tips To Maximize Your Pound Dropping Results in the section below.

Add all the ingredients into your Vitamix or similar high-speed blender. Make sure to add fresh spring water if needed. Add as much water as you like in order to reach your desired thickness of the smoothie.

For all the smoothie recipes, make sure to use organic products, fruits and vegetables if possible.

Blend all the above ingredients until smooth.

Add ice if needed and to your own liking.

You can adjust the raw organic honey to your preference or you can skip this step if you do not have a sweet tooth or if you are following a strict smoothie diet with unsweatened smoothies.

Garnish the smoothie with some organic chocolate chips.

Exotic Green Superpower Ginger & Coconut Smoothie

cucumbers
kale
fresh mint
fresh parsley
fresh ginger
1 avocado
1 cup coconut water
juice of 1 lime
udo's, hemp or flaxseed oil
hemp seeds or chia seeds
liquid stevia

"Not that I loved Ceasar Salads Less, but that I loved Green Smoothies More"

Let's talk about a powerful combination of some fortified, exotic and nutritious superfoods like cucumbers, kale, mint, ginger, coconut water, parsley and more.

The secret ingredient that I use here in order to bring out a rich nutty and exotic tasting flavour is the coconut water.

This is a magical mixture of green and exotic superfoods that are healing in nature. These are ingredients that do not only taste deliciously and exotically, but they will give your body and brain the most nutritious and beneficial nurishment.

Coconut is especially beneficial to help prevent obesity and it improves the heart health.

Coconut is high in dietary fiber, it has a low glycemic index, it reduces sweet cravings, it improves digestion.

It is also a quick energy booster.

In addition, coconut contains no trans fats, it is gluten free and it is non toxic and hypoallergenic.

It also contains antiviral, antibacterial, antifungal, and anti parasitic healing properties.

Coconut helps your overall immune system functions.

Ginger is helping with gastrointestinal relief.

Safe and effective relief of nausea and vomiting during pregnancy.

Ginger carries anti inflammatory effects and helps protect against colorectal cancer.

Ginger induces cell death in ovarian cancer cells and helps boost the immune system.

The Exotic & Green Superpower Smoothie with coconut and ginger contains the following ingredients:

Ingredients:

1-2 organic small cucumbers
3 medium kale leaves (torn)
5 stems of fresh mint
3 stems of fresh parsley
2.5 cm pieces of fresh organic ginger
1 organic avocado
1 cup of organic coconut water
juice of 1 lime
1-2 teaspoons of udo's, hemp or flaxseed oil (optional)
1-2 tablespoons of hemp seeds or chia seeds (optional)
2 - 3 drops of liquid stevia

Directions:

For all these Smoothie recipe simply follow my 5 Minute Easy n'Quick Smoothie Preparation Power Tips To Maximize Your Pound Dropping Results in the section below.

Add all the ingredients into your Vitamix or similar high-speed blender. Make sure to add fresh spring water or ice cubes if needed. Add as much water as you like in order to reach your desired thickness of the smoothie. For all the smoothie recipes, make sure to use organic products, fruits and vegetables if possible.

Mix all the ingredients together and process them with your favorite blender until all of the ingredients are well combined together. Make sure the broccoli is broken down and all the other ingredients are well swirled together in a rich looking creamy texture.

Add a little filtered spring water or ice cubes if needed for your desired consistency.

If you like you can also add some raw honey or if you are on a smoothie diet and like it sweet you can add a little bit of your favorite sweetener.

Other people love the unsweatened taste!

Scrumptious n'Delicious Cherry Choco Drink

Ingredients:
 ½ cup of organic, pitted and stemmed cherries
 1 organic cored and chopped apple
 raw organic cacao powder
 1/2 teaspoon of raw and organic honey

Directions:

Mix all the above organic ingredients in your favorite blender (we recommend the Nutribullet) until everything is deliciously smooth

Better Than A Thousand Donuts Smoothie

5 or 6 frozen banana slices
1 cup frozen fruit
cup vanilla yoghurt
cup milk
1 teaspoon Splenda

"A Green Smoothie is Worth a Thousand Donuts"

A smoothie might be in the blended beverage category, but a smoothie certainly represent very different aspects.

I love the creamy and delicious taste of a smoothie combined with the health benefits that are offered by a smoothie.

All you need is one very secret ingredient that provides the body and brain with a very powerful health benefit and you can turn a simple milkshake into a nutritious drink.

In the case of the Vanilla Smoothie Delight the secret ingredient are frozen bananas.

Did you know that when bananas are frozen and then blended down, they take on the texture of real ice cream?

Yes, real ice cream but without all the dangerous and sick making additives and fats.

In this case I suggest to buy a whole whack of fresh organic bananas. Let them sit out until they have ripened nicely and are yellow.

They should also show some brown spots, but not have gone quite so far as to be in banana bread making material.

Peel your bananas and slice them so that each slice is about 1.5 to 2 centimetres thick.

Separate all the banana slices and lay them flat in a Ziploc bag and place them like this in your freezer.

Avoid throwing them all in at once. They may be hard to break apart in the quantities that you need them later when they are in a frozen condition. Once you have gone through this freezing process, you will have bananas on hand for your smoothie delights for a good amount of time.

This will be a huge time saver because you can live healthy without having to go to the store and buy fresh bananas all the time.

The Vanilla Smoothie Delight is a great smoothie for beginners and you can play around with it and add some of your own variations.

Make sure to write down your own ingredients that you like to add and your preparation method so that you will remember it later.

I suggest using a site like Evernote or a mobile app where you can quickly take all your notes for later reference.

The Vanilla Smoothie Delight is a great recipe that can act as a base for you to build from and it contains the following ingredients:

Ingredients:

5 or 6 small frozen banana slices (organic if possible)

1 cup of frozen fruits (be creative with your selection like peaches, apricots, strawberries, blueberries, blackberries, raspberries, papaya, mango. Make sure the fruits are frozen because this will add to the creamy texture of the smoothie)

¼ cup of organic vanilla yoghurt

½ cup of milk (skim if you are on a strict smoothie diet)

raw honey or splenda (optional and to your liking)

Directions:

For all these Smoothie recipe simply follow my 5 Minute Easy n'Quick Smoothie Preparation Power Tips To Maximize Your Pound Dropping Results in the section below.

Add all the ingredients into your Vitamix or similar high-speed blender. Make sure to add fresh spring water or ice cubes if needed. Add as much water as you like in order to reach your desired thickness of the smoothie. For all the smoothie recipes, make sure to use organic products, fruits and vegetables if possible.

Mix all the ingredients together and process them with your favorite blender until all of the ingredients are well combined together. Blend the frozen slices of bananas and fruits in your favorite blender or food processor on high speed.

You may need to stop occasionally with the process and return some of the fruits to the base of the blender as the fruits can quickly creep up the sides of your mixing bowl.

Keep blending until all the fruits are broken down into a nice smoothie texture.

Next, add in the vanilla yoghurt, the milk and the raw honey or splenda and continue to mix the drink until thoroughly swirled together.

Transfer your drink to a large glass or two smaller ones and enjoy your delicious and nutritious Vanilla Smoothie Delight.

If you need you can also add some more ice cubes or a little filtered spring water depending on your desired consistency.

Chocolate Cocoa Madadamia Coffee Smoothie

Ingredients
   Banana - 2
   Fat free frozen yougurt - 1 cup
   Cold coffee - 1/2 cup
   Almond milk - 1 cup
   Unsweetened cocoa powder - 2 table spoons
   Raw honey to your liking
Topping:
Light whipped cream - 1 cup
Directions:
For all these Smoothie recipe simply follow my 5 Minute Easy n'Quick Smoothie Preparation Power Tips To Maximize Your Pound Dropping Results in the section below.

Add all the ingredients into your Vitamix or similar high-speed blender. Make sure to add fresh spring water if needed. Add as much water as you like in order to reach your desired thickness of the smoothie.

For all the smoothie recipes, make sure to use organic products, fruits and vegetables if possible.

Blend all the above ingredients until smooth.

Add ice if needed and to your own liking.

You can adjust the raw organic honey to your preference or you can skip this step if you do not have a sweet tooth or if you are following a strict smoothie diet with unsweatened smoothies.

Decorate the top with some light whipped cream.

Purple Blue & Vanilla Power Booster

"All Right, Mr. DeMille, I'm Ready for my Purple Smoothie."

Start your day with a smooth start and loading up on lots of protein is a beneficial way to start your day. This smoothie will also give your muscles the perfect energy they need after a tough workout. This smoothie will provide your body with all the nutrients and fuel that it requires.

This protein packed smoothie is loaded with minerals and vitamins. The amount of protein will give you every ounce of energy that you need each and every day.

The Purple Power Booster contains the following ingredients:

Ingredients:

1 cup of purple/blue or vanilla yogurt (blueberry if possible but you can also use vanilla yogurt)

2 cups of frozen purple fruits like blueberries because they are turning this smoothie into a superfood smoothie

1 scoop of vanilla whey protein powder

1 scoop of blueberry flavoured VegeGreens

2 cups of fresh spring water

Directions:

For all these Smoothie recipe simply follow my 5 Minute Easy n'Quick Smoothie Preparation Power Tips To Maximize Your Pound Dropping Results in the section below.

Add all the ingredients into your Vitamix or similar high-speed blender. Make sure to add fresh spring water or ice cubes if needed. Add as much water as you like in order to reach your desired thickness of the smoothie. For all the smoothie recipes, make sure to use organic products, fruits and vegetables if possible.

Mix all the ingredients together and process them with your favorite blender until all of the ingredients are well combined together. Mix all ingredients thoroughly in a food processor or blender.

Add a little filtered spring water or ice cubes if needed for your desired consistency.

Transfer the delicious mix in your favorite smoothie glasses and enjoy.

If you like you can also add some raw honey or if you are on a smoothie diet and like it sweet you can add a little bit of your favorite sweetener.

Some people love the unsweatened and more natural taste.

White Chocolate Macadamia Smoothie

Ingredients:
Unsweetened almond milk - 1 cup
Vanilla greek yogurt (if not available you can even use fat free frozen yogurt) - 1/2 cup
Banana - 1
White chocolate chips - 2 tablespoons
Macadermia nuts - 2 table spoons
Flaxseed (linseed meal) - 1 table spoon
White chia seeds - 1 tea spoon
Cinnamon - 1/2 teaspoon
Ice cubes - 6
Raw honey to your liking

Directions:
For all these Smoothie recipe simply follow my 5 Minute Easy n'Quick Smoothie Preparation Power Tips To Maximize Your Pound Dropping Results in the section below.

Add all the ingredients into your Vitamix or similar high-speed blender. Make sure to add fresh spring water if needed. Add as much water as you like in order to reach your desired thickness of the smoothie.

For all the smoothie recipes, make sure to use organic products, fruits and vegetables if possible.

Blend all the above ingredients until smooth.

Add ice if needed and to your own liking.

You can adjust the raw organic honey to your preference or you can skip this step if you do not have a sweet tooth or if you are following a strict smoothie diet with unsweatened smoothies.

Peanut Butter & Kefir Smoothie

kefir
half a cup of non-fat milk
a frozen banana
peanut butter
some almonds

"What's in a Name? That which we call a Green Smoothie By any Other Name would Taste as Sweet."

This smoothie contains some beneficial ingredients like almonds and kefir.

Almonds are some powerful miracle workers. They are hig in potassium. They also boost your brain activity, reduce the risk of a heart attack and the lower bad cholesterol.

Breakfast is the most important meal of the day.

Make sure not to skip it and consume this powerful breakfast smoothie instead.

This breakfast smoothie is a great way to incorporate nutrition into your day and start your day in an energized and stress free way.

This smoothie delivers a drink that is full of fiber, good carbs and healthy nutrients.

If your goal is to lose weight, I highly recommend to consume this highly nutritionally dense breakfast smoothie every morning during your smoothie diet. It will help you lose weight, keep lean, stave off illnesses, keep clean and boost energy.

This Kefir Peanut Butter Breakfast Smoothie contains the following ingredients:

Ingredients:
1 cup of kefir
some peanut butter for a nutty rich taste
1 organic small banana
a quarter cup of fresh pineapple
1 cup of organic almond milk (self made or bought)

Directions:

For all these Smoothie recipe simply follow my 5 Minute Easy n'Quick Smoothie Preparation Power Tips To Maximize Your Pound Dropping Results in the section below.

Add all the ingredients into your Vitamix or similar high-speed blender. Make sure to add fresh spring water if needed. Add as much water as you like in order to reach your desired thickness of the smoothie. For all the smoothie recipes, make sure to use organic products, fruits and vegetables if possible.

Blend a cup of organic kefir, the peanut butter, a ripe banana, a quarter cup of fresh pineapple and one cup of almond milk and swirl it into a smooth silky treat.

Add ice if needed and to your own liking.

You can adjust some raw organic honey to your preference (if it is not sweat enough for your taste) or you can skip this step if you do not have a sweet tooth.

If you are following a strict smoothie diet, I recommend to keep the Smoothie unsweatened.

If the pineapple is ripe, it will add sugar in a natural way.

Peachy Watermelon Deliciousness

Ingredients:

1 cup of organic and seedless watermelon (remove all the seeds and chop it)

1 organic pitted and chopped peach

½ inch organic and fresh peeled and chopped ginger root

Directions:

Mix all the above organic ingredients in your favorite blender (we recommend the Nutribullet) until everything is deliciously smooth

Purple Vanilla Smoothie

1 peach, frozen
10 blueberries
1 cup light vanilla yogurt
milk
crushed pecan
teaspoons salt
teaspoons vanilla extract

"Round up the Usual Fruits and Vegetables."

The Blueberry Pecan & Vanilla Smoothie is a combination of healthy and lean making superfood ingredients.

So what is the secret of this protein booster?

The secret ingredients are the pecans.

Pecan nuts are a very rich source of energy. Pecans do provide 690 calories / 100 g and do contain health benefiting nutrients: antioxidants, minerals, and vitamins. These are all essential for our wellness.

A regular intake of pecan nuts into your diet plan helps you to decrease total as well as LDL or otherwise known as "bad cholesterol". Eating these nuts does help the increase of HDL or otherwise known as the "good cholesterol" levels in your blood.

Studies also have shown that these healthy compounds that are contained in pecan nuts do in fact help the body remove toxic oxygen free radicals.

This helps protect the body from damages and diseases, infections and cancers.

Pecan nuts do contain anti proliferative properties of ellagic acid which is helping protect the human body from cancers.

Pecan nuts are also an excellent source of vitamin E. Especially rich in gamma tocopherol.

Vitamin E is a powerful lipid soluble antioxidant which is required for maintaining the integrity of cell membrane and Vitamin E helps protect the skin from harmful oxygen free radicals.

These tasty nuts are also a very rich sources of several important B-complex groups of vitamins which are needed for the enzyme metabolism inside the body.

Pecans also do provide a very rich source of minerals like potassium, manganese, calcium, magnesium, iron, magnesium, selenium and zinc.

I recommend to add a hand full of pecans into your smoothies every day to provide your body with sufficient levels of protein, minerals and vitamins.

This protein rich Blueberry Pecan & Vanilla Smoothie contains the following ingredients:

Ingredients:

1 organic peach (frozen)
10-20 organic blueberries (frozen)
1 cup light and fat free organic vanilla yogurt (frozen)
1/2 cup of milk or skim milk
1/2 tablespoon of crushed pecans
1/2 teaspoon of salt
1/4 teaspoons of organic vanilla extract

Directions:

For all these Smoothie recipe simply follow my 5 Minute Easy n'Quick Smoothie Preparation Power Tips To Maximize Your Pound Dropping Results in the section below.

Add all the ingredients into your Vitamix or similar high-speed blender. Make sure to add fresh spring water if needed. Add as much water as you like in order to reach your desired thickness of the smoothie. For all the smoothie recipes, make sure to use organic products, fruits and vegetables if possible.

Put all ingredients into your favorite blender. Blend the mix until your preferred smoothie consistency is reached!

Add ice if needed and to your own liking. You can also add some raw organic honey to your liking or you can skip this step if you do not have a sweet tooth. If you are following a strict smoothie diet, keep the smoothie in its natural and unsweatened form.

Scrumptious Vanilla & Pear Smoothie

Ingredients:
- 1 organic cored and already chopped pear
- 1 organic cored and chopped apple
- 1/8 teaspoon of pure organic vanilla extract
- ½ inch of fresh organic peeled and chopped ginger root

Directions:

Mix all the above organic ingredients in your favorite blender (we recommend the Nutribullet) until everything is deliciously smooth

Green Berry Avalanche

1 large avocado
2 teaspoons condensed milk
1 cup ice
frozen bananas
4 to 5 strawberries
nonfat soy/nut milk
cardamom
allspice

"You had me at 'Green Smoothie." Famous Smoothie Quote

A combination of healthy and lean making avocado and strawberries is what this smoothie's secret is all about.

The avocado is a superfood and strawberries are nutrient-rich and packed with antioxidants. Strawberries provide the body with a rich source of vitamin C and a wide range of health benefits.

Strawberries for example help with wrinkle prevention.

The Mayan Indians have a saying: "Where avocados grow, hunger or malnutrition has no friends."

This antioxidant-rich avocado fruit enhances your heart's health, lowers your cholesterol and improves your skin.

Avocados are abundant in minerals and in vitamins.

Avocados contain beta-carotene, vitamins B6, lutein, vitamins C, E and K, zinc, selenium, potassium, folate, glutathione and omega 3 fatty acids.

These are just a few nutrients that are found in a single avocado.

This Avocado Banana Berry Avalanche is the perfect energy booster if your goal is to follow a lean and clean smoothie diet.

This Avocado Banana Berry Avalanche contains the following ingredients:

Avocado Beauty Recipe:

Mash the pulp of the avocado and apply it directly as a masque to your skin. Avocado contains some of the best anti aging antioxidants and amino acids used in many expensive brand beauty products.

If you suffer from dry skin, spots, sunburn, eczema, or psoriasis, the healthy fat that is contained in avocados is very beneficial for your skin and beauty care because it will heal you from distress, inflammation, dry skin and it will also protect your skin from more damages in the future.

The oil that comes from avocados is the closest to the natural skin oil that is produced by the human body and you can use the avocado pulp and put it on your skin because it has the highest concentration of nutrients.

Just apply it directly to the skin for a soft and supple result.

Ingredients:

1 large organic avocado
2 teaspoons of condensed milk
1 to 1 1/2 frozen organic bananas
5 to 8 frozen or fresh strawberries
a splash of organic non fat soy or other organic nut milk
a pinch of cardamon
a pinch of allspice
ice cubes

Directions:

For all these Smoothie recipe simply follow my 5 Minute Easy n'Quick Smoothie Preparation Power Tips To Maximize Your Pound Dropping Results in the section below.

Add all the ingredients into your Vitamix or similar high-speed blender. Make sure to add fresh spring water if needed. Add as much water as you like in order to reach your desired thickness of the smoothie. For all the smoothie recipes, make sure to use organic products, fruits and vegetables if possible.

Scoop out the avocado fruit into your favorite high speed blender. Add 2 teaspoons of condensed milk. Add the ice cubes and blend all together until you get a a semi creamy and silky texture.

Next add the bananas, the strawberries and the organic non fat soy or nut milk. Finally add the cardamon and the allspice and blend until you reach your desired texture.

I prefer mine very smooth, but some people who tested it prefered a chewable texture of thsi smoothie. You can always add some more ice cubes or fresh spring water to your liking to get the perfect texture.

Delightful Plum Walnut Smoothie

Ingredients:
   3 pitted, chopped and organic plums
   ¼ cup of organic and chopped walnuts
   ½ cup of organic black tea (brew it fresh and then chill it)

Directions:
Mix all the above organic ingredients in your favorite blender (we recommend the Nutribullet) until everything is deliciously smooth

Vanilla Hazel Walnut Cream Smoothie

4 medium bananas
light brown sugar
hazelnuts
1/4 cups milk
1/4 cups dark rum
or hazelnut liqueur
banana liqueur
vanilla syrup
half and half
ice cubes
chopped walnuts

"Hazel Smoothies, I think this is the Beginning of a Beautiful Relationship."

Let's talk about a scrumptious smoothie called the Hazel Banana Vanilla Walnut Cream Smoothie.

It contains some tasty and nutty ingredients like hazelnuts, hazelnut liqueur, banana liqueur, vanilla syrup, and more tasty flavors.

I do not recommend this if you are on a strict smoothie diet, but if you want to treat yourself with a heavenly tasty delight, you must give this one a try.

It contains the following ingredients:

Ingredients:

4 medium bananas (organic if possible and peeled, sliced into 1/2 inch slices)

6 tablespoons of light brown sugar (organic if possible)

1/4 cups of organic hazelnuts

1/4 cup of milk or skim milk

1/4 cups of dark rum or hazelnut liqueur (I prefer the hazelnut liqueur for the nutty taste!)

2 tablespoons of chopped hazelnuts (for the garnish and totally optional)

1 ounce of banana liqueur

1 ounce of vanilla syrup (organic if possible)

2 ounces of half and half

ice cubes

chopped organic walnuts

2 ounces of whipped cream (organic cream if possible)

Directions:

For all these Smoothie recipe simply follow my 5 Minute Easy n'Quick Smoothie Preparation Power Tips To Maximize Your Pound Dropping Results in the section below.

Add all the ingredients into your Vitamix or similar high-speed blender. Make sure to add fresh spring water or ice cubes if needed. Add as much water as you like in order to reach your desired thickness of the smoothie. For all the smoothie recipes, make sure to use organic products, fruits and vegetables if possible.

Place the sliced bananas in a sealed plastic bag and put them back in your freezer and let it freezer for one hour. Place the brown sugar and the hazelnuts in a blender and grind everything together until it is smooth.

Place the frozen bananas, the ice cubes, the milk, the rum or the hazelnut liqueur, the banana liqueur, the vanilla syrup and the half and half in the blender with the brown sugar.

Add ice and blend until smooth

Pour the smoothie drink into your favorite smoothie glasses. Garnish with a topping of whipped cream and sprinkle with chopped hazelnuts and walnuts and serve this tasty delight immediately.

5 Minute Quick Spicy Ginger Smoothie

Ingredients:

1 ripe and small organic banana that is chopped

½ inch of fresh organic, peeled and chopped ginger root

½ tablespoon of raw organic honey

a few ice cubes to your liking

Directions:

Mix all the above organic ingredients in your favorite blender (we recommend the Nutribullet) until everything is deliciously smooth

Boosting Energy With Beta Carotene Smoothie

3 small ice cubes
2 apricots
1/2 papaya
1/2 mango
1/2 cups carrot juice
1 tablespoon honey

"May the Smoothie be with you...Always"

Let's talk about a powerful combination of some fortified, exotic and nutritious orange superfoods like carrots, papaya, mango and more.

The secret ingredient that I use here in order to bring out a rich nutty flavour of this smoothie is the carrot juice that contains a rich source of beta carotene.

This is a magical mixture of orange colored nutritious and healing vegetables and fruits. These are ingredients that do not only taste deliciously, but they will also give your body and brain the most powerful health benefits.

Carrots have a rich supply of antioxidant nutrients called beta carotene.

These delicious orange vegetables are the source not only of beta carotene, but also of a wide variety of antioxidants plus other health supporting nutrients.

Other benefits of carrots are antioxidant benefits, cardiovascular benefits and vision for your health.

The Beta Carotene Energy Booster Smoothie contains the following ingredients:

Ingredients:
2 apricots (sliced and pitted)
1/2 papaya (frozen in chunks)
1/2 mango (frozen in chunks)
1/2 cups carrot juice
1 tablespoon of raw organic honey
3 small ice cubes
Option:
Fresh orange juice

Directions:
For all these Smoothie recipe simply follow my 5 Minute Easy n'Quick Smoothie Preparation Power Tips To Maximize Your Pound Dropping Results in the section below.

Add all the ingredients into your Vitamix or similar high-speed blender. Make sure to add fresh spring water or ice cubes if needed. Add as much water as you like in order to reach your desired thickness of the smoothie. For all the smoothie recipes, make sure to use organic products, fruits and vegetables if possible.

Mix all the ingredients in the order listed together and process them with your favorite high speed blender until all of the ingredients are well combined together. Make sure that everything is broken down and all the ingredients are well swirled together in a rich looking orangy colored texture.

Add the raw honey and blend a few more seconds.

Serve the smoothie in a frosted glass.

Option: If you like a thinner consistency, you can add some fresh orange juice. Add the orange juice and blend everything for one more time.

Like Strawberry Mousse Smoothie

Ingredients for the strawberry mouse
- Avocado - 1 ripe
- Fresh strawberries - 2 1/2 cups
- Chia seeds - 1 tea spoon
- Coconut cream - 1 table spoon
- Raw honey to your liking

Toppings:
- Fresh blueberries
- Goji berries

Directions:

For all these Smoothie recipe simply follow my 5 Minute Easy n'Quick Smoothie Preparation Power Tips To Maximize Your Pound Dropping Results in the section below.

Add all the ingredients into your Vitamix or similar high-speed blender. Make sure to add fresh spring water if needed. Add as much water as you like in order to reach your desired thickness of the smoothie.

For all the smoothie recipes, make sure to use organic products, fruits and vegetables if possible.

Blend all the above ingredients until smooth.

Add ice if needed and to your own liking.

You can adjust the raw organic honey to your preference or you can skip this step if you do not have a sweet tooth or if you are following a strict smoothie diet with unsweatened smoothies.

Top the smoothie with some fresh blueberries and goji berries.

The Triple Blue Energy Triangle

1/2 cups plain or vanilla yogurt
1 1/2 cups frozen blackberries
1 banana
1/2 bag of frozen blueberries
2 tablespoons blueberry preserves
7 or 8 ice cubes
1 1/2 cups of soymilk

"I love the smell of Purple Smoothies in the morning. It Smells like Victory!"

This smoothie contains some beneficial blue, purple and black ingredients like blackberries, blueberries and blue preserve.

There are an unlimited number of variations for this smoothie because you can use different combinations of jams, preserves and fruits.

Maybe you also want to add some protein powder, organic ground flax seed, nuts or any other additional supplements that you prefer.

You can also substitute the organic apple juice for the organic soymilk to make a tangier and more fruity blend.

This makes for the perfect breakfast smoothie to start your day in an energized and stress free way.

The Blackberry Blueberry Blue Preserve Energy Triangle Smoothie contains the following ingredients:

Ingredients:

1 1/2 cups of soymilk
3/4 cups of organic apple juice
1/2 cups plain bio or organic yogurt (I prefer to make my own home-made yogurts)
1 1/2 cups frozen blackberries
1/2 bag of frozen blueberries
2 tablespoons blueberry preserves
1 banana
ice cubes

Directions:

For all these Smoothie recipe simply follow my 5 Minute Easy n'Quick Smoothie Preparation Power Tips To Maximize Your Pound Dropping Results in the section below.

Add all the ingredients into your Vitamix or similar high-speed blender. Make sure to add fresh spring water if needed. Add as much water as you like in order to reach your desired thickness of the smoothie. For all the smoothie recipes, make sure to use organic products, fruits and vegetables if possible.

This is super easy to make. Just put all the ingredients into your high speed blender. Switch the blender to the highest level and blend until you do not hear any ice cubes crunching and until all ingredients are smooth.

Add more ice if needed and to your own liking.

You can adjust the raw organic honey to your preference or you can skip this step if you do not have a sweet tooth or if you are following a strict smoothie diet with unsweatened smoothies.

Green Tea Plum Smoothie

Ingredients:
   3 already pitted and chopped organic plums
   ¼ cup of organic acai berries
   ½ cup of organic and freshly brewed green tea, make sure to chill it first

Directions:
Mix all the above organic ingredients in your favorite blender (we recommend the Nutribullet) until everything is deliciously smooth

The Cinnamon Spice Coffee'n Cream Booster

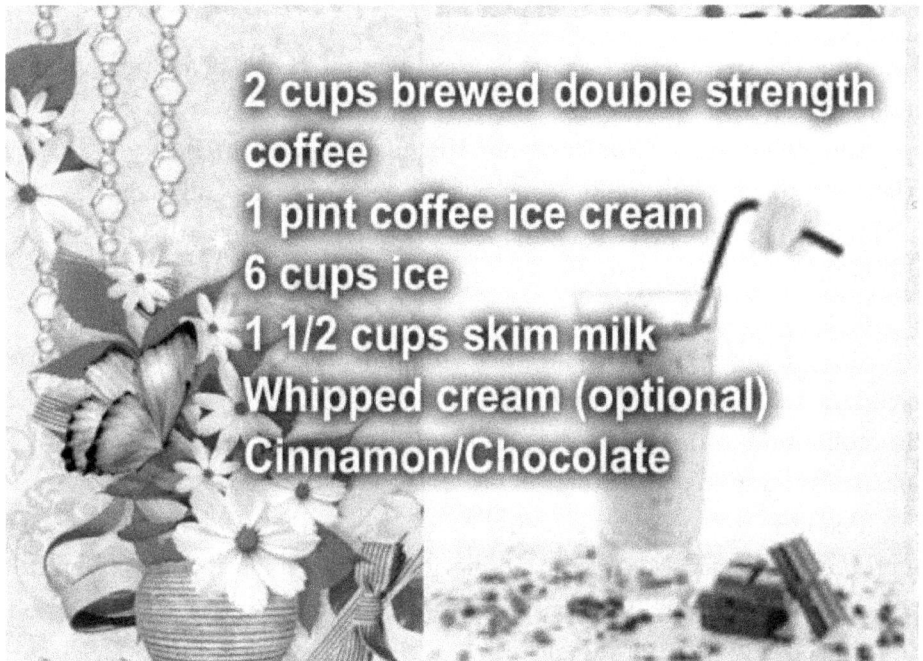

"I'm Going to Make him a Scrumptious Smoothie he can't Refuse."

The secret here is to enjoy the simple but effective blend of a rich tasting coffee in combination with the organic cinnamon and the taste of intelligence maker number one chocolate.

The Coffee'n Cream Cinnamon Smoothie contains the following ingredients:

Ingredients:
2 cups of brewed double strength coffee (organic if possible)
1 pint of coffee ice cream (your favorite brand, I like mine organic)
1 1/2 cups of milk or skim milk
whipped organic cream (as a topping and if desired)
organic cinnamon and chocolate powder for the garnish
6 cups of ice cubes

Directions:

For all these Smoothie recipe simply follow my 5 Minute Easy n'Quick Smoothie Preparation Power Tips To Maximize Your Pound Dropping Results in the section below.

Add all the ingredients into your Vitamix or similar high-speed blender. Make sure to add fresh spring water or ice cubes if needed. Add as much water as you like in order to reach your desired thickness of the smoothie. For all the smoothie recipes, make sure to use organic products, fruits and vegetables if possible.

Mix all the ingredients together and process them with your favorite blender until all of the ingredients are well combined together. Make sure the broccoli is broken down and all the other ingredients are well swirled together in a rich looking creamy texture.

Blend the coffee, the ice cream, the ice cubes and the milk in your favorite high power blender. Mix everything until you get a smooth texture. Top the smoothie with some whipped cream and add some freshly grounded cinnamon and chocolate powder for the garnish.

If you like you can also add some raw honey or if you are on a smoothie diet and like it sweet you can add a little bit of your favorite sweetener.

Other people love the unsweatened taste!

Coconut Almond Smoothie

Ingredients:
   1/2 cup of organic Almond Milk
   1 extra small ripe banana (organic)
   1 organic lime (juiced)
   1/4 cup of organic & salted macadamia nuts
   2 tablespoons of organic cacao nibs
   1 tablespoon of organic coconut palm sugar
   2 teaspoon of cinnamon spice (organic)
   some ice cupes and to your liking
   Raw honey to your liking

Directions:

For all these Smoothie recipe simply follow my 5 Minute Easy n'Quick Smoothie Preparation Power Tips To Maximize Your Pound Dropping Results in the section below.

Add all the ingredients into your Vitamix or similar high-speed blender. Make sure to add fresh spring water if needed. Add as much water as you like in order to reach your desired thickness of the smoothie.

For all the smoothie recipes, make sure to use organic products, fruits and vegetables if possible.

Blend all the above ingredients until smooth.

Add ice if needed and to your own liking.

You can adjust the raw organic honey to your preference or you can skip this step if you do not have a sweet tooth or if you are following a strict smoothie diet with unsweatened smoothies.

The Silky Peanutbutter Banana Smoothie

1/2 cups rice milk
1/2 cups silken tofu
1/3 cups creamy peanut butter
2 fresh bananas

"All Great Things are Simple, and Many can be Expressed in Single Words: Freedom, Justice, Honor, Duty, Mercy, Hope, Smoothies."

Let's talk about this scrumptious Peanutbutter Banana Silk.

Peanuts are not only delicious but they are also very beneficial for the body and brain.

Peanuts are a rich source of antioxidants, they reduced risk of strokes, they help prevent gallstones, they protects against Alzheimer and other age related cognitive decline health problems.

They are very rich in taste and the nutty flavor is popular amongst young and old. As opposed to people's opinion about nuts, they are in fact lowering the risk of weight gain.

The banana is a great combination with peanut butter as Elvis migh confirm because he enjoyed his grand mother's and mother's peanut butter and banana sandwiches. He had too many in order to lose weight, but if you are respecting the ingredient list of this recipe, you are going to enjoy the health benefits of peanut butter in combination with bananas.

Here are some of the main health benefits of the banana. Bananas provide a very beneficial cardiovascular protection because of the potassium and fiber.

Bananas do sooth and protect from ulcers. They also improve elimination and protect your eyesight.

They help with your bones and they do promote kidney health.

The Peanutbutter Banana Silk Smoothie contains the following ingredients:

Ingredients:

1/2 cups of organic rice milk
1/2 cups of organic silken tofu
1/3 cups of creamy organic peanut butter
2 fresh organic bananas (sliced and frozen)
2 tablespoons of dark chocolate syrup
ice cubes

Directions:

For all these Smoothie recipe simply follow my 5 Minute Easy n'Quick Smoothie Preparation Power Tips To Maximize Your Pound Dropping Results in the section below.

Add all the ingredients into your Vitamix or similar high-speed blender. Make sure to add fresh spring water or ice cubes if needed. Add as much water as you like in order to reach your desired thickness of the smoothie. For all the smoothie recipes, make sure to use organic products, fruits and vegetables if possible.

Blend the organic rice milk, the tofu and the organic peanut butter in your favorite high speed blender. Add the banana frozen slices, the dark chocolate syrup and the ice cubes.

Blend on high speed until smooth, about 30 to 50 seconds.

Make sure the ingredients are broken down and all the other ingredients are well swirled together in a rich looking creamy and nutty texture.

Add a little more ice cubes if needed for your desired consistency.

If you like you can also add some raw honey or if you are on a smoothie diet and like it sweet you can add a little bit of your favorite sweetener.

Other people love the unsweatened taste!

Scrumptious Peanut Butter & Apple Smoothie

Ingredients:
  2 organic, cored and chopped apples
  ½ cup of organic apple juice
  2 tablespoons of organic peanut butter
  a pinch of organic cinnamon spice

Directions:

Mix all the above organic ingredients in your favorite blender (we recommend the Nutribullet) until everything is deliciously smooth

The Golden Smoothie Shot

1 apple
1 lemon
1 piece fresh gingerroot
ice
filtered water

"We Are such Stuff As Golden Smoothies are Made of..."

Let's talk about a powerful combination of ginger root, lemon and apple.

The secret ingredient is the ginger root her and let's take a look at what the ginger root can do for you.

The anti inflammatory properties and active principles of the ginger root are thought to provide pain relief in multiple number of ways.

It has the power to stop migraines in their tracks and to ease the aches of arthritis and joint pain.

It also fights ovarian cancer. It seems that ginger has the ability to eliminate the dangerous cancerous ovarian cells. Ginger also seems to slow the progress of bowel cancer.

Ginger also has a boosting effect on the immune system, making you fit and healthy.

Make sure to consume this immune system boosting smoothie drink on a daily basis to stay healthy and clean all year around!

I suggest to drink this smoothie in slow sips and you can keep it near your workspace so you can take a sip throughout the day. If you have trouble sleeping than make sure to only drink this secret ingredient drink in the morning because ginger has a similar characteristic as coffeine.

The Peanutbutter Banana Silk Smoothie contains the following ingredients:

Ingredients:
1 organic small apple (peeled, cored, sliced)
1 organic lemon (peeled, seeded)
1/2 cups of fresh filtered source water
ice cubes
1 piece of fresh gingerroot (peeled, crushed)

Directions:
For all these Smoothie recipe simply follow my 5 Minute Easy n'Quick Smoothie Preparation Power Tips To Maximize Your Pound Dropping Results in the section below.

Add all the ingredients into your Vitamix or similar high-speed blender. Make sure to add fresh spring water or ice cubes if needed. Add as much water as you like in order to reach your desired thickness of the smoothie. For all the smoothie recipes, make sure to use organic products, fruits and vegetables if possible.

Mix all the ingredients together and process them with your favorite blender until all of the ingredients are well combined together. Blend all ingredients together until smooth.

Make sure to drink the Golden Delight slowly.

Add a little filtered spring water or ice cubes if needed for your desired consistency.

If you like you can also add some raw honey or if you are on a smoothie diet and like it sweet you can add a little bit of your favorite sweetener.

Other people love the unsweatened taste!

Delicious Green Greek Yogurt Smoothie

If you love to get the health benefits from spinach, but do not really like the taste, make sure to try this smoothie. It is delicious because you can not really taste the spinach. You can almost not see the spinach neither.

For this recipe you can use whatever milk is your favorite. I love this recipe particularly with vanilla coconut milk, but you can use rice, hemp, almond, dairy, or soy milk alternatively.

I love to add raw organic honey, pure maple syrup, or agave nectar. Sometimes a little touch of organic vanilla extract also works fine.

Ingredients
   2/3 cup of organic plain creamy Greek yogurt
   1 small organic ripe banana
   2/3 cup of fresh or frozen blueberries (organic if possible)
   2 large fresh or frozen strawberries (organic if possible)
   1 cup of fresh or frozen spinach leaves (organic if possible)
   1/2 cup of fresh organic milk (alternatively you can also use rice, hemp, coconut, soy, vanilla coconut milk, and almond milk)
   2 teaspoons of protein powder (this is totally optional)
   1 tablespoon of raw organic honey

Directions:

For all these Smoothie recipe simply follow my 5 Minute Easy n'Quick Smoothie Preparation Power Tips To Maximize Your Pound Dropping Results in the section below.

Add all the ingredients into your Vitamix or similar high-speed blender. Make sure to add fresh spring water or ice cubes if needed. Add as much water as you like in order to reach your desired thickness of the smoothie. For all the smoothie recipes, make sure to use organic dairy products, vegetables and fruits if possible.

Blend everything in your favorite high speed blender.

Blend on high speed until smooth, about 30 to 50 seconds.

Make sure the ingredients are broken down and all the other ingredients are well swirled together in a rich looking creamy and nutty texture.

Add a little more ice cubes if needed for your desired consistency.

If you like you can also add some raw honey or if you are on a smoothie diet and like it sweet you can add a little bit of your favorite sweetener.

Some great natural sweetening options are: agave, raw honey, and maple syrup. Use the organic brands if possible.

5 Minute Easy n'Quick Smoothie Preparation Power Tips To Maximize Your Pound Dropping Results

These are some pro tips you can apply to these healthy smoothies to make your weight management even more pound dropping:

Be sure to pour in liquids first and more solid ingredients last.

Start from the lowest speed of your blender and work up your way to the highest speed once the blend smoothes out. Add ice or fresh source water last, and use as much or as little as you'd like.

I suggest using 3 cubes of ice for each smoothie, but it is fine to add more and make the smoothie a little slushier to attain a creamier texture. Some of my smoothies use cow's milk, or dairy free subs like coconut; almond, hemp, soy and rice milk.

Pick your favourite milk or make a mix of your own preference.

If you have leftover smoothie mix, distribute it into an ice cube tray for simple mixing next time.

Top smoothies with some eye catching decorations like fresh slices of fruit, sliced nuts, seeds, unsweatened dark organic chocolate, or shredded coconut.

Try making a ritual out of your smoothie diet and consume an oatmeal, orange, flax seed, and pineapple smoothie every day.

Freeze fruit for a heavier consistency or use frozen fruits form the market. Make sure to never spare on quality ingredients. Use organic ingredients if possible.

Chop up your ingredients before starting the mixing process.

9 Tips How To Turn A Smoothie Diet Experience Into Living The Smoothie Lifestyle

1. Blend a couple of times a day and as long as you plan to apply your Smoothie diet.

2. Combine it with eating healthy clean foods for 1 meal and a healthy snack or two throughout the day.

3. Combine your smoothie diet with a light daily workout ritual like Yoga or any other physical activity.

4. The more smoothies you drink during the day and the less processed foods you consume the more weight you are going to lose.

5. Don't push yourself too hard. This is a long term strategy and once you reached your dieting goal, make sure to include these healthy smoothies into your daily meal plan in order to stay fit and keep a lean body.

6. Reward yourself with some scumptious and healthy Paleo desserts and guilt free baked goods or a nice tea ceremony or anything else you are interested in like listening to good music, watching an interesting movie, experiencing mindfulness, developing your mental state, etc.

7. Never abuse anything and keep the balance

8. Always motivate yourself and stay on the positive side of things. When things get tough get clarity via meditation, yoga, breathing techniques and bliss

9. Respect these rules above on a daily basis and applying a daily Smoothie ritual in combination with juicing and a light healthy meal plan and workout is going to be transformational and life changing for your health, mind and seoul. This process is also called living the Smoothie Lifestyle which should be your ultimate goal if you desire to double your life and stay lean and clean.

10 Step Smoothie Diet/Smoothie Lifestyle Method

"There are two primary choices in life: to accept conditions as they exist, or accept the responsibility for changing them." ~Dr. Denis Waitley

10 Step Smoothie Diet/Smoothie Lifestyle Method For Maximum Pound Dropping Results

The most serious merit of using smoothies for dropping pounds is they make you full. When you cutting back on calories, it is perfectly natural and fine that you are going to feel hungry. It is tough not to focus on food items when you are hungry. For many dieters, chewing on food leads to over indulging which in turns results in sensations of inadequacy. Incadequacy then might lead to a failed diet.

A healthy and well combined smoothie will steer you to feel full. If you do not feel very hungry, you are not thinking about eating all the time and you will be achieving more successful and more fulfilling results.

When you also consider that some ingredients can also aid in promoting weight loss, smoothies are the best break when trying to drop pounds. I am constantly and consistently trying new weight loss smoothie recipes and methods to personalize my smoothie lifestyle.

These are my propositions for making changes and for making these healthy Smoothies far more effective for my smoothie lifestyle. The following are some handy tips that will help you with maximizing your weight loss results with the power of smoothies.

Ingredient 1: Kefir or Nonfat Yogurt or Sherbert

Use fat-free yogurt or kefir. This is blazingly clear, but it is vital to assert. If the smoothie recipe calls for ice cream, you can substitute it with frozen and fat free yogurt or sherbert. Again, I love vanilla flavor so I typically use vanilla-flavored yogurt with no fat. You can use Italian sherbert like unsweatened and non fat lemon sherbert. You can also make it yourself without sugar or with raw honey.

Ingredient 2: Milk Alternatives

Almonds are a great addition if your aim is to consume smoothies for weight control. Soy milk has only seven grams of sugar per cup. Cow milk has about twelve grams per cup. One cup of soy milk has about eighty calories. Soy milk and dairy milk have a matching amount of protein and carbohydrates.

Nevertheless fortified soy milk have larger amounts of what is called omega-fats (healthy for your heart), isoflavones and micronutrients. It raises the level of high density of lipoproteins (HDL) in the blood stream and also decreases the amount of triglycerides and low density lipoproteins (LDL). It is possible to get some vanilla soy milk. Vanilla soy milk makes your smoothies for weight control much more tasty and enjoyable.

Almonds are heavey in fat. This helps lead you to feel full and satisfied. The Omega-3 trans-acids help reduce your body's fat. It also helps increase the amount of lean muscle tissue. Complete flax seeds do add a nice nut flavor and a nutty texture. Flax seeds also add extra micronutrients and fiber. You will try playing with other seeds, nuts and grains to find your favorite. Diet fiber leads you to feel full. It also takes more time to eat and digest fiber, which helps combat overindulging and overeating. This is the reason why you need to add more fiber to your smoothies. Particularly if you are using smoothies for the purposes of dropping pounds make sure to add lots of fiber ingredients. Raspberry fruits, as an example, taste wonderful and raspberries have about eight grams of diet fiber per cup.

Making use of the whole raspberry fruit if feasible will also add to your smoothie's fiber content.

With some fruit, like apples, the skin is very healthy to add to the smoothie. In most fruits, the stem; the seeds, the core, and the pits might contain valuable nutriments so make sure to add these fruits. Do not be troubled that they will make your smoothie taste very bad. Should you happen to have a correct blender like my favorite Vitamix or any other alternative, everything will get mixed and combined so well into your diet smoothie that you will not notice they are there.

Ingredient 3: Oranges, Lemons, Grapefruits...

Sour citrus fruits tend to have lots of polyphenolic acids which are good anti oxidizing compounds for your body. If you do not really like the taste, don't cut them out of the smoothie recipe. As an alternative add a small amount of raw honey to sweeten your smoothies.

Ingredient 4: Exotic Fruits

Organic ananas and pineapple juice are the commonest ingredients in my smoothie lifestyle.

Not only are these ingredients easy to get access to because almost any supermarket has a good selection, but both ingredients are cheap in relation to other more expensive fruits like papaya and mango.

Both ingredients contain further nutrient elements and go with virtually any smoothie recipe (a mix of bananas and / or pineapple with vanilla equals a superb taste). In fact if you don't wish to add any artificial sweatener or raw honey, you want to use pineapple juice to naturally sweeten up your smoothie recipes. Pineapple juices are a great source of potassium and vitamin C. It is also rich in Thiamine. Thiamine is a soluble type of vitamin that is in the vitamin B group. Thiamine also helps convert carbohydrates into energy, helping maintain a good nervesystem, insightfulness and clearness. If you can prepare whole pineapple fruits instead of bottled or canned fruit juices for your weight control smoothies, you should always give your priority and preference to whole, fresh and organic fruits.

Most fruit juices are so highly processed that there's little left in them except sugar, taste and color. Making use of the whole fruits instead of the bottled juices will make sure you get the maximum nutrient elements and the highest health benefits.

I am really not a nourishment expert or dietician, so I am not going to go into all the health benefits here, but always remember that some fresh fruits are much better than others. Apply this info when you substitute some of your ingredinets with other fruits because this knowledge is important for your smoothie diet.

Ingredient 5: Super Boosters

If you can always use superfruits in your smoothies. These fruits include but are not limited to: goji fruits, red guava, strawberries, oranges, papaya, cherries, mango, goji, blueberries and kiwi solely to name a couple so make sure to always include these super fruits.

Some studies have suggested that vitamin C assists in minimizing fat deposition. Replace your yogurt and your milk consumption with the following ingredients: almonds, avocado, cashew nuts, coconut oil and add ice or water to adjust the thickness to your liking.

Ultimately, to my mind smoothies should be a fast and entertaining way to load up on nutrient elements in a convenient and tasty way so that you can meet your weight loss goals in a very effective way.

Ingredient 6: Greens

Go with fresh green plant smoothies, fruit juices and healthy salads.

To keep your salads plain, you can wash the lettuce and chop the cucumber and some carrots.

It is usually possible to revolve the veg and non-sweet fruits to balance your intake. You may also add some raisins or berries together with seeds and natural dressings.

Ingredient 7: Variety

For most events, just pick out at least four recipes you can make for the entire week and eat the same food a day or two in a row.

If you're thinking this is dull, you are definitely wrong. The food will be so fresh and tasty that you can not imagine only having one meal of a recipe, so try more portions of it in a week.

For example if this week you are having a plant burger for lunch, make it as the key dish of your dinner for a couple of days. Later on make an enormous crop of plant salads, which may likely last for 2 lunches and a dinner.

Since the last time you made falafel, put some in the refrigerator, and take out your break composed from cut veggies like carrots or celery to make it plain. If you're having an intensely busy week just have some plant smoothies to sustain your diet without even troubling with the kitchen.

Ingredient 8: Plan Your Smoothie Diet

Keep a once-a-week menu that's pre-planned for a month or two. You can jot it down, with more details for your breakfasts, nibbles, lunch, dinners, snacks, etc.

At least have a special book or a little pocket notebook where you can note down all of your plans, together with ticklers, post-it notes, coloured pens and some stickers to add character to your organizer.

By writing each plan and what you eat, you can give more time to anticipate, as well as enough reason to maintain the way of life. And, it could also help in motivating yourself to prepare your smoothies. Once it's all planned, most work will be simpler. The more that you add green smoothies to your way of life, the less you may want for unhealthy food.

Make a habit of thinking around the quality ingredients that you need to include in your smoothies and plan these ingredients into your smoothie plan while keeping your preferred fruits and vegetables at all time.

Ingredient 9: Timing - Only 5 Minutes Or Less

My guideline is if I'll make a good smoothie in five minutes or less and if it tastes heavenly on top of it, I keep the recipe in my collection of smoothies for weight control and for my smoothie lifestyle. If it is taking me more than five minutes and if it is too difficult to make and apply, I do not even bother and do not consider it. If a recipe takes too long to make it is not practical and I won't make it again for productiveness reasons.

The smoothie lifestyle is all about quick and easy five minute smoothie recipes that are tasty and healthy.

If I adore the taste of it I attempt to give it an opportunity and try experimenting with the ingredients by removing various ingredients or preparation steps till I'm pleased and satisfied with the substitutes and the time factor and the taste factor.

I love the formula of five minute fast while the recipe is still packed with maximum nutrient contents for the maximum healthy benefits.

All of the recipes that are included in this book have been tested and they are all proven. All the recipes that are included in this book went through my five minute test. All of the recipes do fit my five minute fast preparation formula and all of them do qualify.

I know from experience and from interactions with my clients that the time factor plays a critical role when it comes to keeping a dieting program realistic and result driven.

Today's life complexities and time restrictions continually challenge us to think up new productiveness and productivity strategies. Following work and social life challenges us to continually finetune our consumption habits and a similar thing is applicable to following a certain way of life or a diet. This is the reason why I only include smoothies that fit the five minute preparation ritual.

It is easy enough to follow and this is what I call a result driven and practical diet.

Ingredient 10: Live The Smoothie Lifestyle

In my viewpoint why the smoothie diet is so effective is really because the following formula applies:

1. Five minute preparation time
2. Deliciousness of the smoothies
3. The Blend of these nutrient elements is healthy and constructive for the body and brain
4. Empowerment of an approach to life with smoothies rather than a unrealistic and failing diet that leads to another failing diet and the vicious circle begins

There are that many intense and counter productive diets that work against the body rather than with the intelligence of the body. These unhealthy and fad diets just don't work because they're lacking all the pieces (or at a minimum one of the pieces) that are included in the smoothie diet formula above.

This smoothie diet is a kind, stressfree, tasty, fun, healthy and delightful diet. It's a productive diet because not only are the smoothies five minute fast to make, but you don't feel hungry all of the time and you can achieve your jobs without considering food all of the time. The nutrient elements that are included in these smoothies are very strong for the body and brain and they're stimulating the body and brain to function in a productive and advantageous way.

This in turn motivates you, encourages you, enables you and empowers you to adhere to take action and live a smoothie life-style (a way of life not a diet). Such a healthy and enjoable lifestyle will in turn aid you in keeping and maintain a lean and clean body and mind. This connection is the final goal of a succesful smoothie diet or better yet smoothie lifestyle.

Now it's time to start with these healthy and exquisite smoothies and it's your call to cause it to happen.

Take action today and take all the action steps.

Include the smoothie lifestyle into your life and give your body and mind clean and healthful food so that you can become a lean and clean you and double your life starting with today.

Scrumptious & Healthy Pound Dropping Juices

Juices detoxify the body system. Juicing gives you a strong dosis of nutrients and vitamins and minerals.

Juicing can even help you lose weight and maintain a healthy living.

Let's dive right into what the juicing lifestyle has to offer to you!

My Favorite Quote About The Juicing Lifestyle

"Juices of fruits and vegetables are pure gifts from Mother Nature and the most natural way to heal your body and make yourself whole again." — Farnoosh Brock

Why Drinking Juices Is Important

Juicing is beneficial to your health, but what if you're looking to juice for a specific health benefit? Find and choose the benefit you're looking to juice for below!

Applying a daily juicing ritual will help with the following:

Weight Loss (I lost 40lbs within a period of 2 month by combining my Secret Morning Elexir, Juicing, Smoothies and a light mealplan)

Antioxidants

Alzheimer's Prevention

Asthma Help (I suffered for years from breathing problems and Asthma and finally was able to get rid of it because of my daily Juicing and Smoothie ritual)

Blood Cleanse

Arthritis Prevention

Bone Protection

Cancer Prevention

Cervical Cancer Prevention

Breast Cancer Prevention

Colon Cancer Prevention

Liver Cancer Prevention

Lung Cancer Prevention

Prostate Cancer Prevention

Cataracts Prevention

Ovarian Cancer Prevention

Stomach Cancer Prevention

Digestion

Detoxification

Energy

Digestion

Heart Disease Prevention

Immune System

Hydration

Improving Eyesight

Improved Complexion
Increased Blood Circulation
Kidney Cleanse
Increased Libido
Liver Cleanse
Lower Blood Pressure
Lower Cholesterol
Macular Degeneration Prevention
Mental Health
Osteoporosis Prevention
Pain Relief
Reduce Inflammation
Reduce Water Retention
Stroke Prevention

More Benefits From Applying A Daily Juicing Habit:

Increase in energy and alertness as well as a renewed sense overall health and vigor

When you lean the art of juicing you can enjoy delicious and freshly made fruit and veggie juices to boost your system

Enjoy drinking morning boosting juices to get your day started and to be ready to face new challenges

Play with all kinds of flavors and combinations of ingredients in order to find the one combination that you simply can not live without anymore

You can say no to sick making preservatives, chemicals, additives, and yes to natural sweeteners and a wonderful flavor experience

Discover all kinds of juices that you can make and use for other things like:

Freezing your own juices for later usage

Use your homemade juices for your own self-made cooking and baking recipes like pies, breads, soups, sauces, muffins, cakes and many other delicious treats

The juice makes an excellent stock or natural source of sweetener and they are much easier for the body to process than refined sugars

When you really put your mind to juicing, I imagine you will be amazed by all the wonderful uses you can find with these magical, healthy and healing juices

Welcome to the wonderful and magical world of juicing!

Healing & Detoxifiying Your Body With Wheat Grass Juices

Wheat grass is simply put a young wheat plant. Wheat grass is widely consumed in liquid form by health conscious people who prefer the concentrated rich source of enzymes, minerals and vitamins.

The main aspect that makes these wheat grass juices so healthy is the fact that it contains chlorophyll.

Nearly 70% of wheat grass is chlorophyll. Some individual state that a small pound of wheat grass is equal to 20 pounds of fresh garden greens! This is just one of the reason why health fans are liquefying this grass and drinking it.

Wheat grass juice is quickly rising to the top of the favorite juices.

It retains most of the essential minerals. These minearls, enzymes and vitamins are promoting health and help repair cell damage.

Wheat grass juice also has the ability to increase oxygenation in the human body plus it helps build up the red blood cells. These red blood cells are the carriers of oxygen to the body's cells. In addition it purifies our blood and organs while destroying the nasty toxins. In general, wheat grass is a true metabolism booster.

Wheat grass juice is the perfect replacement for dark green leafy vegetables that you should supplement your diet with.

Wheatgrass is also a very rich source of alkalinity for the body. It is often found in supplemental form so that you can mix it with water and drink it if you do not have an adequate juicer that can process wheat grass. Some fans choose to drink a daily glass of fresh wheatgrass juice to insure that their body is getting enough alkaline forming food.

Juicers can break down the cellulose barriers and extract all of the juice inside fruits, grasses and veggies.

However, you should know that not all juicers are capable of making real wheat grass juice.

If you try to juice wheat grass in a juicer that is not made to process grass, you will probably end up with a damaged or clogged juicer.

The best juicers for wheat grass are those that are multipurpose juicers. These multipurpose juicers will not only make juices from veggies and fruits, but you can apply them to make wheat grass.

If you have any questions, simply ask lots of questions before buying your juicer.

You may want to purchase a wheat grass juicer if you plan to only process grass. These juicers are also known as single auger juicers. They are crushing the grass while squeezing out all of the rich chlorophyll juice of the grass.

Newer models of these single auger juicers do include two levels. The first level works to crush the grass and squeeze out the healthy juice while the second level pulls the remaining pulp through a second crushing and extraction process.

Today you can find many models of these auger or juice extractors. Do not let buying a juicer get in your way. Simply identify what type of juicer you want by determining what type of ingredients you want to process.

Remember, when you get into the habit of drinking healthy wheat grass juice, you should go step by step and start out slowly because the taste of the wheat juice migh surprise you at first.

I did not like the taste at all when I got started, but learned how to integrate these healthy green juices into my daily juicing ritual.

I started by drinking one ounce per day and slowly work my way up to three ounces per day which is ther perfect amount in order to get the most nutritious value into the system of the body.

You will see that such a habit will bring long term health and a clean and lean body!

5 Minute 6 Step Juice Fasting System For Busy People

Step by Step Instructions For Juicing

For all these juicing recipe simply follow my 5 minute step by step instructions.

Step 1

Wash all veggies and fruits. Going through this thorough cleaning process will help prevent a nasty food-borne disease. I love to use organic vinegar because it is the most natural and organic solution, buy there are other options available if you prefer using products that are specifically designed for washing vegetables and fruits.

Step 2

Peel and cut all your fruits and veggies. Remember, you are juicing raw vegetables. This is why you need to cut them into small pieces before you get started. Especially if you are applying crunchier fruits and veggies such as carrots. Some high speed or high power juicers or a combination of juicer/blender like the Vitamix are able to take veggies and fruits in their whole form. In this case just follow the manufacturer's manual. Peel the skin of all your veggies and fruits. You also need to peel fruits like apples, melons, bananas, papaya, mango, pineapple, kiwis, banans, avocados, etc.

Next cut and chop the fruits and veggies such as leafy greens and fruits.

Step 3

Put your fruits and veggies into your favorite juicer or blender or a combination of juicer/blender (Nutribullet) and strictly follow the directions of the manual that comes with your machine. The manual will tell you what buttons to puch and what speed to use.

Juice the softer fruits/textures first.

You will see that when you are juicing the crunchier veggies and fruits they will help you push the softer and more delicate fruits and veggies through the blades.

If you are not using a juicer and only have a blender available, make sure to first strain the juice from citrus fruits like oranges, lemons, grapefruit, etc.

When you are finished you can either leave the pulp inside the juice or take it out. It is totally up to your preference.

Next add the juice back to your mixture in the blender and proceed from there.

Step 4:

Juice and blend everything together as per instructions from your manual. You can always add some raw honey or sweatener depending on your goal with these juices. If the juice is too strong for you, you might also add some ice cubes or source water.

I only add ice cubes and water to smoothies, but some friends of mine who got started with juicing told me that some of the juices were too strong for them and they added ice cubes or water. In the summer time, ice cubes might be a refreshing alternative.

You will see that experimenting with your juicing process will help you discover many varieties and alternatives which makes juicing such a fun and exciting experience.

Step 5:

Try a variety of fruit and vegetable mixtures. As you experiment with juicing, you will find many combinations that you will enjoy on a daily basis. Some that pair well include apples with carrots, and leafy greens with kiwi. Try anything you want to taste. Create several go to recipes for yourself that you can use to make a healthy habit out of juicing.

Step 6:

The last step is a very important one if you want to enjoy your juicer/blender for a very long time.

Make sure to clean your machine ASAP and once you are done with your juice.

This helps prevent nasty bacteria growth and in order to prevent any diseases that related to hygiene.

Use warm water and dish soap. You can also use vinegar to clean and then run the pieces through the dishwasher.

If you do not have a dishwahser take extra care with the cleaning process.

Step 7:

Make sure to add lots of fiber to your smoothies, eat whole fruits and veggies throughout the day in order to stay balanced otherwise you might risk a dietary deficiency.

Step 8:

Enjoy your refreshing and delicious juice!

Step 9:

Refer to chapter Juicing For Weight Loss if your only goal is to lose weight with juicing.

Why You Should Consider A High Speed Juicer

In my opinion the Breville Speed Juice Extractor is one of the most powerful juicers that money can buy. I have used mine for quite some while and it has never once let me down.

I reckognize that there is a big choice of juicers available on the market because juicing has become such a popular topic.

I know that it can become a challenging process to decide which juicer is most valuable for your purposes.

I can only tell you from my own experience that the Breville BJE510XL Ikon Juicer is the best choice that I made because it has consistently performed better and more effective than the other juicers that I have been testing on a continuous basis for myself and for my clients.

The Breville is by far one of the best juice extractors on the market today and offers the best quality for the investment. Below you will find some characteristics that might be of interest for you if you are thinking about investing into a quality juicer yourself.

If you do not have the funds in the beginning of getting started with your juicing lifestyle, you can always use some alternative or manual juice aids in combination with your blender.

It does not have to be expensive to get started with juicing and you can always use the more affordable solutions to get results first.

Juicing Performance Of The Breville

You want to make sure that your juicer is able to extract juice from fruits and veggies without leaving much of excess pulp behind. The Breville BJE510XL will perform in this respect. It extracts only the optimal amount of nutritious juice from veggies and fruits.

Ikon Jucier Overview of The Breville:

900 watts
Measures 16 x 9 x 16 inches
5-speed system
Speeds range from 6500 rpm to 12500 rpm
Weighs 9 pounds

Volume Level Of The Breville:

The Breville seems to generate the same amount of noise as the competitors like the Green Star Juicer and others.

The noise will depend on your individual noice tolerance. You can expect it to make the same level of noise as an average juicer or blender.

Speed Of The Breville:

The Breville BJE510XL is designed with a speed control. The speed of the machine can be adapted to the veggies and fruits that are used. When you are juicing with the Breville, veggies and soft fruits do require a slower speed than firmer and crunchier fruits and veggies like broccoli. The Breville is designed with a control that allows you to effectively run the machine at exactly the right speed to get the most out of the juice.

It is designed to use the minimum effort to achieve the maximum results. The Breville also comes with a user friendly manual. The manual tells you the exact speed that you should set for each ingredient. This gives you the maximum output of juice and a minimum of messing around.

Juicer Design Of The Breville:

The Breville has a large shoot. It is spacious enough to fit several carrots or a whole apple in at a time. This reduces the time you can spend and it takes away the tedious tasks of slicing, dicing and chopping.

This juicer is something you are going to be proud to show off in your home. It has a very sleek and stainless steel finishing which will complement almost any home decor. The classy design earned a designer prize, the Australian Design Award.

Another feature of the Breville which contributes to the look is the fact that it will not stain after usage. Many juicers become discolored after usage, but the Breville BJE510XL is easy to clean and always returns into its original appearance after usage.

The Breville Juicer comes with several parts. It creates a firm seal when all the parts are snapped together. The juicer comes with a bright LCD screen. The LCD screen shows your current settings with fruit icons. This will guide you to select the matching speed for each ingredient.

What Comes With The Breville?

When you buy the Breville juicer you get a manual, a juice jug, a detachable spout, a froth separator and a cleaning brush.

Clean Up Of The Breville

Many consumers do love the Breville juicer because it is especially easy to clean up. When it is running, you will notice that all of the pulp is deposited into a separate container. If this seperate container is lined with plastic, it will quickly and easily be able to be emptied out. The various parts of the Breville juicer easily disassemble and fit easily into your dishwasher.

Warranty Of The Breville?

1 year of replacement warranty comes with the Breville BJE510XL juicer.

Since I want to make a healthy diet and a healthy lifestyle achievable and affordable for real people in real life, I went ahead and created a collection of juice recipes just for people who already invested in the Breville or who are going to invest in it in the near future in order to better their life.

As stated earlier you can apply all the recipes by using a more affordable juicer or a manual solution and you do not have to invest in an expensive high speed juicer to make this work for you.

The upcoming collection of juices has been created with the Breville juicer. I created these Breville juicing recipes for real people that have one goal in mind: Getting started with a realistic healthy diet and a healthy lifestyle like the fast juicing diet because they know it is achievable if action is taken on a daily basis.

Let's get started with the scrumptious & healthy juicing recipes that you can quickly and easily make with your own Breville juicer or with an affordable alternative juicing aid, too!

Secret Elixir Juice Fasting Ritual To Maximize Pound Dropping Results (Do This First Thing In The Morning)

I had to find out a different way to lose weight because no diet worked on me. Finally with these detoxing and fat burning juices that I have created via my juicing weight loss program I was finally able to have success and was able to rebooted my system.

Today I am able to keep off the 40 lbs that I lost with my juicing diet because I am respecting my juicing ritual. It is not hard anymore like it was when I first tried to lose weight.

Here is my lemon elixir that I drink every morning before I have my first juice.

Ingredients:

1 cup of warm or room temperature source water

Juice from 1 lemon (organic if possible)

1 teaspoon of raw apple cider vinegar

A pinch of cinnamon

1 teaspoon of raw honey (alternatively you can also use a couple drops of stevia)

For example, you can use stevia if you are on a yeast cleansing diet or low sugar diet.

I drink this every morning, whether I am "feasting" or not, this is my morning coffee and I enjoy my morning elixir ritual!

What this morning elexir ritual does for you:

This morning elexir stimulates digestion and it releases toxins from the liver. It also jump starts your digestive enzymes.

Benefits of this morning lemon elexir ritual:

Raw honey benefits:

* Raw honey is loaded with minerals, vitamins & enzymes

* It helps cleanse your liver, flushes out fat from your body when done first thing in the morning on an empty stomach and remove toxins

* Raw honey soothes indigestion (it relieves acidity in your stomach)

* Energy booster

* Anti microbial and anti fungal

* Raw honey helps to keep your skin clear (it helps with skin conditions such as ring worms, eczema & psoriasis)

Apple Cider benefits:

* Apple Cider is a natural remedy for heartburn
* It can help clear up your skin conditions and acne
* It promotes digestion and apple cider will keep you regular
* Apple cider helps control weight
* It can help regulate your blood sugar
* Apple Cider helps reduce sinus infections and sore throats
* It is very rich in potassium and enzymes
* It can help ease menstrual cramps
* It also helps promote youthful healthy bodies and skin

Lemon benefits:

* Lemon helps make the body more alkaline (increases pH)

* It provides lots of Vitamin C

* It purifies your blood and detoxes you

* Lemon is a cleansing agent & tonic for your liver by helping it produce more bile

Immune System Boosting Pomegranate Juice

Drinking fruit and veggie juices on a daily basis is a exciting, scrumptious, quick and easy way to boost the immune system. Green juices provide antioxidants and other nutrients. These help the body maintain a healthy and strong immunological defense perimeter.

The Pomegranate contains lots of different vitamins like vitamin C and betacarotene. This awesome fruit also contains folic acid. Folic acid is essential to produce the healthy red blood cells and it prevents anemia (a lack of haemoglobin).

Here is the Pomegranate Mint Juice that is not only beneficial to your immune system as an immune system booster, but it is also super scrumptious in taste.

This Pomegranate Mint Juice is providing all the essential flavonoids, vitamins and other essential nutrients to your body.

This in turn helps maintain a healthy and happy lifestyle!

You'll see this is a fresh & tasty juice that is going to ensure your body maintains hydrated while getting loads of minerals and vitamins at the same time.

Ingredients:
1 Pomegranate (orgnic if possible)
50 g of fresh Mango (orgnic if possible)
2 fresh and organic mint stalks

some ice cubes

Directions:

Peel the pomegranate and remove its seeds

Peel your fresh mango

Put mango and pomegranate in your favorite blender or your favorite juice press.

Pour your juice in your favorite juice glass and add the fresh washed mint and the pomegranate seeds on top of it

Plain 4 OJ

Ingredients:

4 medium sized oranges and if possible organic

Go ahead an juice the oranges and usual and remember that you should keep as much of the white membranes as possible.

Doing so will give you a huge advantage because the white stuff is rich in bio-flavonoid

If the juice is too sour or unpleasant in taste, go ahead and add some organic raw honey to make it sweeter in taste

Triple Green Beauty Drink

1 Handful of Kale or Spinach
2 Cucumbers
1 Granny Smith Apple
Lime
Ginger

This is my secret green beauty juice and I make sure to mix it into my daily meal plan because I enjoy the beautifying benefits of it. It really makes my skin soft, hydrated and wrinkle free. I add some powerful organic and self made beauty products for my skin care and this is all I need to stay beautiful from the inside out.

I am working on a new series where I divulge my skin care and beauty secrets and you can soon check them out and add them to your home spa and beauty program, too.

A combination of juices and smoothies, the benefits from my self made beauty and skin care system and a light yoga and meditation workout is all I need in order to create the ultimate healthy lifestyle for myself and my family.

The green beauty juice is a fortified and nutritious combination of healthy and lean making superfood greens like kale, cucumbers and spinach.

Mixing nutritious veggies like kale and spinach and fruits like apples and lime will bring a sweat taste to this juice because fruits help neutralize strong and bitter flavours that might come from the veggies.

The ginger gives this juice drink some powerful health benefits like immune boosting actions.

The reason kale is becoming popular is because it helps you fill up without a lot of calories to speak of. It doesn't have any fat, has plenty of fiber as well as iron and Vitamin K. Because of its antioxidant content you'll get anti-inflammatory benefits which helps to reduce the symptoms of inflammation, while also helping to avoid the rise of certain diseases. It also helps to restore and maintain an alkaline state.

This Green Beauty Juice contains the following ingredients:

Ingredients:
1 handful of either Kale or Spinach (organic if possible)
2 cucumbers (organic if possible)
1 apple (granny smiths are the best because I have tried out everything)
1/2 Lime (organic if possible)
1/4" ginger

Directions:
For all these For the directions please refer to the chapter where I am talking about my 5 Minute 6 Step Juicing System.

Here is a short instruction that sums up what to do. Make sure to refer back to my 6 step process for juicing so that you get the whole idea of juicing.

In this case peel the cucumbers, apple, lime and ginger.

Next cut and chop the fruits and veggies.

Put all the fruits and veggies from the ingredients list into your favorite juicer or blender or a combination of juicer/blender (Nutribullet) and strictly follow the directions of the manual that comes with your machine.

The manual will tell you what buttons to puch and what speed to use.

Juice the softer fruits/textures first.

You will see that when you are juicing the crunchier veggies and fruits they will help you push the softer and more delicate fruits and veggies through the blades.

If you are not using a juicer and only have a blender available, make sure to first strain the juice from the lemon.

Once it is finished you can either leave the pulp inside or take it out. This is totally up to your preference.

In this case you have to add the juice back to the blender and proceed from there.

Juice and Blend the juices with the other ingredients from the list above together as per instructions.

You can always add some raw honey or sweatener depending on your goal with these juices. If the juice is too strong for you, you might also add some ice cubes or source water.

Enjoy your refreshing Green Beauty Juice that will beautify you from the inside out!

Power Ginger Parsley Lemon Cocktail

The ingredients of this powerful juice are all very beneficial for the body and brain.

Spinach is one of the most nutrient dense packed foods you can provide your body with. It proves you with energy. Spinach helps you fill your stomach without adding a lot of calories and you feel satisfied and full.

Spinach contains phytonutrients that are working as antioxidants battling against the free radical damage.

By consuming spinach you are helping to nourish your body on a cellular level.

Spinach is a great ingredinet for weight loss juices.

Spinach is also an alkaline powerhouse. Baby spinach is great, too. Since there are so many other alkalizing vegetables out there, I recommend trying out different variations and concoct a juice that will send your pH levels to the sky.

This is also the reason why I love combining spinach and kale or baby spinach with spinach and kale.

The health benefits of celery are very powerful, too. In addition to being an alkaline food, celery is very low in calories and it is a great weight loss ingredient for juicing if weight loss is on your mind.

Celery is a great combination as a third ingredient because it brings even more health benefits to the table.

I always love to add celery into fruit based juices as well because it adds a bit of spiciness without overshadowing the sweet flavors of the fruits.

Experimenting with and knowing the benefits of all these ingredients is key to a successful juicing experience.

Parsley is the third green raw ingredient that powers up this juice drink to the next level. Parsley also helps keep your body alkaline. This green herb is not only powering up your juice with lots of health nutrients, but it helps bring out the freshest taste ever. It freshes up the taste of your juice because it adds more vitamins and minerals to your juice.

The great thing is that you can grow your own parsley pretty easily at home and always have it ready to freshen up your juices, smoothies and other recipes that you are making.

I only grow my own parsley and include it in most of my juicing drinks.

The fourth green ingredient of this power packed juice is the cucumber. The cucumber is a heavy hitter. I always keep a good stock of cucumbers at home. Cucumbers are alkaline, and they do contain so much water that it is a very hydrating vegetable.

As you can see this juicing drink is a loaded with powerful greens that you can mix up and find lots of variations that might work for you. I just add some zesty ginger, orange and lemon to this power cocktail which makes the bitter taste of the celery sweeter and perfect for a healthy morning and breakfast juice with a zest.

The Green Orange Breakfast Power Cocktail contains the following ingredients:

Ingredients:
4 Stalks of celery (organic if possible)
1 Cup of Spinach or baby spinach (organic if possible)
2 Cucumber (organic if possible)
1 Orange (organic if possible)
Few sprigs of parsley (organic if possible)

1 small knob of ginger (organic if possible)

1 lemon (organic if possible)

Directions:

For all these juice recipe For the directions please refer to the chapter where I am talking about my 5 Minute 6 Step Juicing System.

Here is a short instruction that sums up what to do. Make sure to refer back to my 6 step process for juicing so that you get the whole idea of juicing.

In this case peel the lemons, limes, carrots, and beet (or buy prepared).

Next cut and chop the fruits and veggies.

Put all the fruits and veggies from the ingredients list into your favorite juicer or blender or a combination of juicer/blender (Nutribullet) and strictly follow the directions of the manual that comes with your machine.

The manual will tell you what buttons to puch and what speed to use.

Juice the softer fruits/textures first.

You will see that when you are juicing the crunchier veggies and fruits they will help you push the softer and more delicate fruits and veggies through the blades.

If you are not using a juicer and only have a blender available, make sure to first strain the juice from the lemon and orange.

Once it is finished you can either leave the pulp inside or take it out. This is totally up to your preference.

In this case you have to add the juice back to the blender and proceed from there.

Juice and Blend the juices with the other ingredients from the list above together as per instructions.

You can always add some raw honey or sweatener depending on your goal with these juices. If the juice is too strong for you, you might also add some ice cubes or source water.

Enjoy your Orange Juice Detoxifier!

Green Juicing Recipe With Kale & Spinach

Ingredients:
1 fresh handful kale leaves (stemmed and organic if possible)
1 fresh handful romaine (hearts and organic if possible)
1 handful fresh spinach leaves (orgnic if possible)
2 handfuls of fresh and organic parsley leaves
2 1/2 fresh and organic celery stalks
1 fresh and peeled ginger (one piece)
1/2 squeezed lemon juice (organic if possible)

Directions:
Wash all the ingredients
Cut up your ingredients as needed to fit through the chute of your favorite juicer
Juice all the ingredients except your lemon juice
Add the lemon juice
Serve the juice immediately and enjoy this green health booster!

3 Apples A Day Keeps The Doctor Away Juice

If you are a beginner in juicing this one is what you should get started with.

Pouring the contents of delightful oranges and green fruits and veggies into my favorite blender (in my case I am using the Nutribullet because it juices and keeps the pulp in the glass plus it also makes my favorite smoothies) and whipping everything together into a zesty healthy green elexir is what I loved most when I got started with jucing. The experience of making these healthy delights is unmatched and it got me very excited and involved when I first got started with juicing.

This zesty Powerful Beginner's Juice contains the following ingredients:

Ingredients:
Apples - 3 medium and preferably organic (3" dia)
Celery - 4 stalks, large and preferably organic (11"-12" long)
Fresh Ginger - 1/4 thumb (1" dia)
Lemon organic (with rind if organic) - 1/2 fruit (2-1/8" dia)

Orange (for juicing and peeled) - 1 large (3-1/16" dia)

Spinach - 5 cups and organic if possible

Directions:

For the directions please refer to the chapter where I am talking about my 5 Minute 6 Step Juicing System.

Here is a short instruction that sums up what to do. Make sure to refer back to my 6 step process for juicing so that you get the whole idea of juicing.

In this case peel the apples, ginger, lemon if not organic and orange.

Next cut and chop the fruits and veggies.

Put all the fruits and veggies from the ingredients list into your favorite juicer or blender or a combination of juicer/blender (Nutribullet) and strictly follow the directions of the manual that comes with your machine.

The manual will tell you what buttons to puch and what speed to use.

Juice the softer fruits/textures first.

You will see that when you are juicing the crunchier veggies and fruits they will help you push the softer and more delicate fruits and veggies through the blades.

If you are not using a juicer and only have a blender available, make sure to first strain the juice from the lemon and orange.

Once it is finished you can either leave the pulp inside or take it out. This is totally up to your preference.

In this case you have to add the juice back to the blender and proceed from there.

Juice and Blend the juices with the other ingredients together as per instructions.

You can always add some raw honey or sweatener depending on your goal with these juices. If the juice is too strong for you, you might also add some ice cubes or source water.

Enjoy your refreshing and delicious Powerful Beginner's Juice!

Zesty Ruby Juice

If you love tasty juices with some weird secret ingredient combinations that are super healthy and taste deliciously, consider the Apple Carrot Beet Trianon juice elexir.

Pouring the contents of a delightful apple, green and red veggies into your favorite blender and whip it all together into a zesty elexir that will supply your body with a cocktail full of these healthy nutrients is part of my daily juicing ritual.

This zesty Green & Red Health Elexir contains the following ingredients:

Ingredients:
  2 Carrot (organic if possible)
  1 Apple (organic if possible)
  6 Celery Ribs (organic if possible)
  1 Beet (small and organic if possible)
  1 hand full of cilantro and/or parsley and/or cilantro

1" size slice of ginger (organic if possible)

Directions:

For all these juice recipe For the directions please refer to the chapter where I am talking about my 5 Minute 6 Step Juicing System.

Here is a short instruction that sums up what to do. Make sure to refer back to my 6 step process for juicing so that you get the whole idea of juicing.

In this case peel the beets (or buy them already prepared and ready to use), apple, carrots and ginger.

Next cut and chop the fruits and veggies.

Put all the fruits and veggies from the ingredients list into your favorite juicer or blender or a combination of juicer/blender (Nutribullet) and strictly follow the directions of the manual that comes with your machine.

The manual will tell you what buttons to puch and what speed to use.

Juice the softer fruits/textures first.

You will see that when you are juicing the crunchier veggies and fruits they will help you push the softer and more delicate fruits and veggies through the blades.

Juice and blend all the ingredients from the list above together as per instructions.

You can always add some raw honey or sweatener depending on your goal with these juices. If the juice is too strong for you, you might also add some ice cubes or source water.

Enjoy the Apple Carrot Beet Trianon!

Triple Citrus Immunity System Booster

This is my secret citrus beauty juice and I make sure to mix it into my daily meal plan because it helped me control my Asthma and breathing problems.

The secret combination of grapefruit, lemon and organges is what makes this juice a Vitamin C booster.

It is a is also a great liver detoxifier.

In a condition of insufficient oxygen and breathing problems (mountain climbing, etc.) lemons are very helpful.

I suffered from Asthma and breating problems and have been able to get rid of it by changing by eating and drinking habits. Drinking this juice is part of my daily juicing ritual.

Vitamin C in lemons for example helps the body to neutralize free radicals that are linked to most types of diseases and aging.

This Citrus Immunity Booster is a winner and it contains the following ingredients:

Ingredients:
1 Grapefruit, organic if possible and peeled

1 Lemon (organic if possible and you can keep the rind if organic)
3 Oranges (juicing organges and peeled)
1 large slice of pineapple (preferabley fresh or canned)

Directions:

For the directions please refer to the chapter where I am talking about my 5 Minute 6 Step Juicing System.

Here is a short instruction that sums up what to do. Make sure to refer back to my 6 step process for juicing so that you get the whole idea of juicing.

In this case peel the grapefruit, the lemon, the oranges and the pineapple.

Next cut and chop the fruits.

Put your fruits into your favorite juicer or blender or a combination of juicer/blender (Nutribullet) and strictly follow the directions of the manual that comes with your machine.

The manual will tell you what buttons to puch and what speed to use.

Juice the softer fruits/textures first.

You will see that when you are juicing the crunchier veggies and fruits they will help you push the softer and more delicate fruits and veggies through the blades.

If you are not using a juicer and only have a blender available, make sure to first strain the juice from the oranges, grapefruit and lemon.

Once it is finished you can either leave the pulp inside or take it out. This is totally up to your preference.

In this case you have to add the juices back to the blender and proceed from there.

Juice and Blend the juices with the pineapple together as per instructions.

You can always add some raw honey or sweatener depending on your goal with these juices. If the juice is too strong for you, you might also add some ice cubes or source water.

Enjoy your refreshing and delicious juice!

Zesty Apple Lemonade

Ingredients:
2 fresh and organic apples
The juice of one organic lemon
1" slice of an organic ginger root

This juice is a very healthy remedy for colds (lemon is rich of vitamine C and apples generally keep the doctor way). Make sure to drink this specific health elexir during the cold winter times to prevent any colds.

This juice is rich in flavonoid content.

The Zestyu Apple Lemonade has a fresh tangy taste which is yet another benefit of this health elexir.

When drinking this juice every morning during the cold winter months, I feel quite invigorated and full of energy and I highly recommend to make this juice part of your daily juicing ritual because it is truly effective to fight any colds and it is not expensive to make in relation to what it does for your body. You can keep a bunch of apples, lemons and ginger in stock for one whole week and like this you do not run out of ingredients so quickly.

I always make it my goal to get stock for one whole week so I do not have to run out all the time during the coldest months of the winter.

Happy Orange Carrot Juice

A combination of healthy and lean making kale and spinach is what this smoothie is all about. The Everyday Go To Juice is a perfect solution if your goal is to follow a lean and clean juicing diet.

So what is so beneficial about the Everyday Go To Juice power booster?

The secret ingredient of Kale. Kale contains a rich source of antioxidant related health benefits. It also contains glucosinolates which provide the body with cancer preventive benefits.

Kale also provides you with detox activating isothiocyanates and cardiovascular support.

I have tested this juice with a lot of friends and family members before adding it to my favorite collection of juices. They all got some great benefits out of drinking this Everyday Go To Juice on a daily basis.

I am constantly testing and proving new juicing recipes that I am gradually adding to my "Tested & Proven Juicing Recipe Collection"

This one has passed the test because it is not only delicious, but it is such a health treat and perfect for you if you are trying to lose weight with juices.

Spinach, kale and celery might not sound appealing to you at first, but the combination of all the ingredients is turning this juice into an absolute winner. It does not only taste deliciously, but it provides your body and brain with a powerful mix of rejuvenating and healing nutrition.

This Everyday Go To Juice drink contains the following ingredients:

Ingredients:

1 large handful of organic spinach and organic kale (if you do not have both available just use one of them)

1 bunch of celery (organic if possible)

3 cucumbers (organic if possible)

8 carrots (organic if possible)

2 green apples (organic if possible)

2 oranges (juicing oranges)

1/2 inch ginger

Directions:

For the directions please refer to the chapter where I am talking about my 5 Minute 6 Step Juicing System.

Here is a short instruction that sums up what to do. Make sure to refer back to my 6 step process for juicing so that you get the whole idea of juicing.

In this case peel the cucumbers, carrots, apples, oranges and ginger.

Next cut and chop the fruits and veggies.

Put all the fruits and veggies from the ingredients list into your favorite juicer or blender or a combination of juicer/blender (Nutribullet) and strictly follow the directions of the manual that comes with your machine.

The manual will tell you what buttons to puch and what speed to use.

Juice the softer fruits/textures first.

You will see that when you are juicing the crunchier veggies and fruits they will help you push the softer and more delicate fruits and veggies through the blades.

If you are not using a juicer and only have a blender available, make sure to first strain the juice from the oranges.

Once it is finished you can either leave the pulp inside or take it out. This is totally up to your preference.

In this case you have to add the juice back to the blender and proceed from there.

Juice and Blend the juices with the other ingredients together as per instructions.

You can always add some raw honey or sweatener depending on your goal with these juices. If the juice is too strong for you, you might also add some ice cubes or source water.

Enjoy your refreshing and delicious Everyday Go To Juice!

Exotic Lychee Leafy Green Drink

The nutritional benefits of lychees is very valuable because lychees are very rich in Vitamin C. Did you know that hundred grams contain approximately 100% of the daily dose of Vitamin C?

Lychees are a great source of phosphorous, copper, and potassium. The two main antioxidants that can be found in lychee fruits do include anthocyanins and polyphenols.

Lychees also add a very exotic and delicate taste to the smoothie.

Lychee fruits are wonderful to combine with other tropical fruits like passion fruits and pineapple.

Lychees work best paired with mild tasting leafy greens.

Go for slightly firm lychees that are not too ripe because like this the green smoothie tastes best.

Ingredients:

9 organic lychee (peeled and deseeded) - if you do not get them fresh you can also use organic canned brands

1 medium banana (organic if possible and peeled)

1/2 cup of organic pineapple (cubed)

2 cups of fresh baby spinach (organic if possible)

6 ounces of fresh filtered water or bottled source water

Directions:

For all these Smoothie recipe simply follow my 5 minute directions. Add all the ingredients into your Vitamix or similar high-speed blender. Make sure to add fresh spring water or ice cubes if needed. Add as much water as you like in order to reach your desired thickness of the smoothie. For all the smoothie recipes, make sure to use organic products, fruits and vegetables if possible.

Blend everything in your favorite high speed blender.

Blend on high speed until smooth, about 30 to 50 seconds.

Make sure the ingredients are broken down and all the other ingredients are well swirled together in a rich looking creamy and nutty texture.

Add a little more ice cubes if needed for your desired consistency.

If you like you can also add some raw honey or if you are on a smoothie diet and like it sweet you can add a little bit of your favorite sweetener.

CCOG Power

If you love tasty juices with some powerful orange ingredients that are super healthy for your eye sight and taste deliciously, then you might consider the Orange Eye Health Elexir.

Carrots have a rich supply of antioxidant nutrients called beta carotene. Carrots will supply your body with antioxidant benefits, cardiovascular benefits and they boost your visions health.

Pouring the contents of a delightful oranges, cucumbers, carrots and ginger into your favorite blender (in my case I am using the Nutribullet because I love its versatillity) and whip it all together into a zesty elixir that heals and keeps your eyes healthy.

This zesty Orange Eye Elixir contains the following ingredients:

Ingredients:
   9 carrots (organic is best)
   2 cucumbers (organic is best)

2 fresh juice oranges

1"ginger (the secret ingredient)

Directions:

For the directions please refer to the chapter where I am talking about my 5 Minute 6 Step Juicing System.

Here is a short instruction that sums up what to do. Make sure to refer back to my 6 step process for juicing so that you get the whole idea of juicing.

In this case peel the cucumbers, carrots, oranges and ginger.

Next cut and chop the fruits and veggies.

Put all the fruits and veggies from the ingredients list into your favorite juicer or blender or a combination of juicer/blender (Nutribullet) and strictly follow the directions of the manual that comes with your machine.

The manual will tell you what buttons to puch and what speed to use.

Juice the softer fruits/textures first.

You will see that when you are juicing the crunchier veggies and fruits they will help you push the softer and more delicate fruits and veggies through the blades.

If you are not using a juicer and only have a blender available, make sure to first strain the juice from the oranges.

Once it is finished you can either leave the pulp inside or take it out. This is totally up to your preference.

In this case you have to add the juice back to the blender and proceed from there.

Juice and Blend the juices with the other ingredients from the list above together as per instructions.

You can always add some raw honey or sweatener depending on your goal with these juices. If the juice is too strong for you, you might also add some ice cubes or source water.

Enjoy your refreshing Orange Eye Health Elexir that will beautify you from the inside out!

Alkaline Juice

Ingredients:
  1 cup of fresh organic spinach (frozen if not possible otherwise)
  ½ cup of organic cucumber
  2 stalks of organic celery plus the leaves
  3 organic peeled carrots
  ½ peeled organic apple

Directions:

For the directions please refer to the chapter where I am talking about my 5 Minute 6 Step Juicing System.

Here is a short instruction that sums up what to do. Make sure to refer back to my 6 step process for juicing so that you get the whole idea of juicing.

In this case peel the cucumber (or buy them already prepared and ready to use) and carrots and apple.

Next cut and chop up all the veggies and fruits.

Put all the veggies from the ingredients list into your favorite juicer or blender or a combination of juicer/blender (Nutribullet) and strictly follow the directions of the manual that comes with your machine.

The manual will tell you what buttons to puch and what speed to use.

Juice the softer veggie textures first. You will see that when you are juicing the crunchier veggies first they will help you push the softer and more delicate ones through the blades.

Juice and Blend all the ingredients from the list above together as per instructions.

Enjoy this regenerating Alkaline Juice!

Remember the skin of a dark cucumber is going to provide you with the source of chlorophyll which is a phytochemical. This can help build up your red blood cells in your body.

The cucumbers do contain silica as well which is a mineral source that is very good if you want to achieve a youthful looking skin

Detoxifying Juice Bomb

Who says that vegetables are for lunch and dinner only? This leafy green and lean cocktail contains delicious and zesty fruits that are swirled into the greens and this smoothie makes for a perfect wholesome and healthy start of your day so that you do not need to wait for lunchtime to eat these healthy veggies.

It does not only taste deliciously, but kale provides the body with anti inflammatory health benefits. The Vitamin C of the lemon detoxifies your body and destroy intestinal worms and the carrots are helping your eye sight. Just to name a few health benefits that come with this detoxifying drink.

This Detoxifying Juice contains the following ingredients:
Ingredients:
9 Carrots (organic if possible)
1 large handful of organic spinach or lettuce of your preference
1 large handful of kale (organic if possible)
1 lemon (organic if possible)
Directions:

For the directions please refer to the chapter where I am talking about my 5 Minute 6 Step Juicing System.

Here is a short instruction that sums up what to do. Make sure to refer back to my 6 step process for juicing so that you get the whole idea of juicing.

In this case peel the carrots and lemon.

Next cut and chop the fruits and veggies.

Put all the fruits and veggies from the ingredients list into your favorite juicer or blender or a combination of juicer/blender (Nutribullet) and strictly follow the directions of the manual that comes with your machine.

The manual will tell you what buttons to puch and what speed to use.

Juice the softer fruits/textures first.

You will see that when you are juicing the crunchier veggies and fruits they will help you push the softer and more delicate fruits and veggies through the blades.

If you are not using a juicer and only have a blender available, make sure to first strain the juice from the lemon.

Once it is finished you can either leave the pulp inside or take it out. This is totally up to your preference.

In this case you have to add the juice back to the blender and proceed from there.

Juice and Blend the juices with the other ingredients from the list above together as per instructions.

You can always add some raw honey or sweatener depending on your goal with these juices. If the juice is too strong for you, you might also add some ice cubes or source water.

Enjoy your Detoxifying Juice that will burn the fat and detox your body!

Beet Lemon Celery Drink

This is a fortified and nutritious combination of healthy and lean making raw greens like celery and red/orange raw foods such as beets and carrots.

This juice gets its rich flavour from the mix of green red and orang raw foods.

Who says that vegetables are for lunch and dinner only? This lean green cocktail contains delicious and zesty lemon that is swirled into the juice.

This juice makes for a perfect wholesome and healthy start of your day so that you do not need to wait for lunchtime to eat these healthy veggies.

If you feel that the juice is too strong or too bitter, you can always add an juicy apple into the blend to make it sweeter in taste.

I enjoy it with apples as a breakfast juice and without apples as a lunch or dinner option.

The Beet Juice Booster contains the following ingredients:

Ingredients:
2 beets (organic if possible)
6 carrots (organic if possible)

2 stalks of celery (organic if possible)

1/2 lemon (organic if possible)

apples (depending on your own preference and time of the day)

Directions:

For all these juice recipe For the directions please refer to the chapter where I am talking about my 5 Minute 6 Step Juicing System.

Here is a short instruction that sums up what to do. Make sure to refer back to my 6 step process for juicing so that you get the whole idea of juicing.

In this case peel the beets (or buy them already prepared and ready to use), carrots and lemon.

Next cut and chop the fruits and veggies.

Put all the fruits and veggies from the ingredients list into your favorite juicer or blender or a combination of juicer/blender (Nutribullet) and strictly follow the directions of the manual that comes with your machine.

The manual will tell you what buttons to puch and what speed to use.

Juice the softer fruits/textures first.

You will see that when you are juicing the crunchier veggies and fruits they will help you push the softer and more delicate fruits and veggies through the blades.

If you are not using a juicer and only have a blender available, make sure to first strain the juice from the lemon.

Once it is finished you can either leave the pulp inside or take it out. This is totally up to your preference.

In this case you have to add the juice back to the blender and proceed from there.

Juice and Blend the juices with the other ingredients from the list above together as per instructions.

You can always add some raw honey or sweatener depending on your goal with these juices. If the juice is too strong for you, you might also add some ice cubes or source water.

Enjoy your Beet Juice Booster!

Pomegranate Health Elexir

Ingredients:

5 pomegranates

To make this as healthy as possibe we are only using the seeds of this powerful fruit.

You discarded everything else

You will need your favorite blender to break down the seeds first

Juicing Process:

Go ahead and put all your pomegranate seeds into your favorite blender. I am using the Nutribullet for this process.

Mix the seeds a few times help them break apart and release the pomegranates juice

Do not blend them for a long time

The seeds will break apart and create cloudy juice which we don't want to happen

Next, use a mesh strainer

Strain the pomegranate juice into a storage container

Use the back of a spoon or other alternative kitchen tool

Push it against the pomegranate pulp

Extract as much of liquid from the seeds as possible

Chill the juice in the fridge

Enjoy this wonderfully tasting and healthy elexir and get the maximum health benefit out of it

Strawberry Beet Kale Goodness

Let's talk about a powerful combination of some fortified and nutritious red/orange superfoods like carrots, beets, strawberries and green superfoods.

The secret of this juice is the combination of the red/orange superfoods together with the greens.

This is a magical mixture of orange and green nutritious and healing vegetables and fruits. These are ingredients that do not only taste deliciously, but they will also give your body and brain the most powerful health benefits.

Carrots have a rich supply of antioxidant nutrients called beta carotene.

These delicious orange vegetables are the source not only of beta carotene, but also of a wide variety of antioxidants plus other health supporting nutrients.

Other benefits of carrots are antioxidant benefits, cardiovascular benefits and vision for your health.

The real benefit of strawberris is that they are tasting great and that they are providing enough nutrients to the body.

Strawberries provide a boost to your immune system. They helps your eyes and they help fight cancer. They also helps with cholesterol and with inflammation. They also have anti-aging properties.

The mix of greens combined with orange and red raw fruits and veggies is what makes this juice so special.

The Beet Strawberry Carrot Empowerer contains the following ingredients:

Ingredients:
1 beet (organic if possible)
4 carrots (organic if possible)
1 cup of strawberries (organic if possible)
6-8 kale leaves (organic if possible)
3 cucumbers (organic if possible)

Directions:
For all these juice recipe For the directions please refer to the chapter where I am talking about my 5 Minute 6 Step Juicing System.

Here is a short instruction that sums up what to do. Make sure to refer back to my 6 step process for juicing so that you get the whole idea of juicing.

In this case peel the beet (or buy already prepared and ready to use), carrots and cucumbers.

Next cut and chop the fruits and veggies.

Put all the fruits and veggies from the ingredients list into your favorite juicer or blender or a combination of juicer/blender (Nutribullet) and strictly follow the directions of the manual that comes with your machine.

The manual will tell you what buttons to puch and what speed to use.

Juice the softer fruits/textures first.

You will see that when you are juicing the crunchier veggies and fruits they will help you push the softer and more delicate fruits and veggies through the blades.

Juice and Blend all the ingredients from the list above together as per instructions.

You can always add some raw honey or sweatener depending on your goal with these juices. If the juice is too strong for you, you might also add some ice cubes or source water.

Enjoy the delicious Beet Strawberry Carrot Empowerer!

Mouth Watering Mango & Mint Juice

Ingredients:
    1 organic, peeled and chopped mango
    ½ inch organic, peeled and chopped raw fresh ginger root
    1 teaspoon organic and chopped mint
    ½ teaspoon fresh squeezed organic lime juice

Directions:

Mix all the above organic ingredients in your favorite blender (I recommend the Nutribullet) until everything is deliciously juicy!

Clean Out Your Body Juice

The liver cleanser juice contains a combination of healthy and lean making cucumbers, beets and carrots. This combination is what this juice is all about.

The beets, carrots and cucumber are all nutrient-rich and packed with antioxidants and this is what makes this juice so powerful. This drink is a true immune system booster. It also is a powerful liver cleanse and detox drink because it cleans your system and makes it toxin free.

Beets provide the body with a rich source of Vitamin C and a wide range of other health benefits. The beetroot also contains folate and this helps prevent cancer and heart diseases.

The carrots enhance your vision health. Carrots provide you with a rich supply of antioxidant nutrients called beta carotene.

Cucumbers contain so much water that it is a very hydrating vegetable which combines very well with the healing benefits of the beet and the carrots.

This hydrating Liver Cleanser Juice is the perfect power booster for hot summer days, in the morning and whenever your body needs a good supply of hydratation and it contains the following ingredients:

Ingredients:
6 carrots (organic if possible)
1 beet (organic if possible)
1 cucumber (organic if possible)

Directions:
For the directions please refer to the chapter where I am talking about my 5 Minute 6 Step Juicing System.

Here is a short instruction that sums up what to do. Make sure to refer back to my 6 step process for juicing so that you get the whole idea of juicing.

In this case peel the beets (or buy them already prepared and ready to use), carrots and cucumber.

Next cut and chop the veggies.

Put all the veggies from the ingredients list into your favorite juicer or blender or a combination of juicer/blender (Nutribullet) and strictly follow the directions of the manual that comes with your machine.

The manual will tell you what buttons to puch and what speed to use.

Juice the softer veggie textures first. You will see that when you are juicing the crunchier veggies first they will help you push the softer and more delicate ones through the blades.

Juice and Blend all the ingredients from the list above together as per instructions.

Enjoy this refreshing Liver Cleanser Juice!

Quick n'Easy To Fix Strawberry Plum Drink

Ingredients:

2 pitted and already chopped organic plums (fresh or packaged)

3 fresh or frozen organic strawberries (make sure they are stemmed and already chopped)

¼ teaspoon of freshly squeezed organic lime juice

½ cup of organic and unsweetened apple juice

Directions:

Mix all the above organic ingredients in your favorite blender (we recommend the Nutribullet) until everything is deliciously smooth

Super Food Juice

Let's talk about a powerful combination of ginger root, celery, spinach, kale, cucumbers and apples.

The secret ingredient of this juice is the ginger root. Let's take a look at what the ginger root can do for you.

The anti inflammatory properties and active principles of the ginger root are thought to provide pain relief in multiple number of ways.

It has the power to stop migraines in their tracks and to ease the aches of arthritis and joint pain.

It also fights ovarian cancer. It seems that ginger has the ability to eliminate the dangerous cancerous ovarian cells. Ginger also seems to slow the progress of bowel cancer.

Ginger also has a boosting effect on the immune system, making you fit and healthy.

Make sure to consume this immune system boosting smoothie drink on a daily basis to stay healthy and clean all year around!

I suggest to drink this juice in slow sips and you can keep it near your workspace so you can take a sip throughout the day.

Ginger also improves your breath. It can cleanse the palate leaving your mouth feeling refreshed.

Ginger protects against nuclear radiation and if you want to get the full benefits of this advantage you will have to consume a daily dose.

Ginger also strengthens your immunity. An improved immune system can mean that you get ill less often. It means that you will recover quicker. It also means that when everyone else around you is coming down with something you can stay fit and healthy.

Ginger also fights cancers. Ginger has been shown to help treat various forms of cancer, including ovarian cancer.

Ginger protects against Alzheimer's disease.

Ginger helps to slow down the loss of brain cells that typically is the precursor to Alzheimer's disease.

Ginger is perfect for weight loss because it stimulates the appetite. If you have a very sluggish digestive system and find out that you need to get your digestive fire going before eating a meal, ginger can help you out.

Ginger can also help as an appetite stimulant to get your digestive juices flowing so that you are better able to digest foods and lose weight as a side effect because improper digestion of food leaves the food fermenting in your digestive system which can lead to weight gain as a side effect.

Ginger is a fat burning superfood and it acts as a fat burner. Ginger helps you feel satisfied and full. This means that you will eat less food which will help reducing your overall caloric intake in the end.

Ginger is a true magical secret ingredient and this juice combines ginger and turns it into an even healthier raw power cocktail.

I am enjoying the benefits of ginger every day. If I do not have enough time to make a juice because I am pressed in time, I consume at least a glass of ginger water or ginger tea with lemon.

If you are looking to lose weight like I did, you make sure to drink a glass of this magical ginger water or ginger/lemon water (cold or hot as herbal tea) throughout the day and in little sips. If you apply this ginger water method you will always feel full and satisfied.

This Leafy Green Super Food Juice contains the following ingredients:

Ingredients:
- 6 leaves Kale (organic if possible)
- 2 cups Spinach (organic if possible)
- 2 Cucumbers (organic if possible)
- 4 stalks Celery (organic if possible)
- 2 apples (organic if possible)
- 1" ginger root (organic if possible)

Directions:

For all these juice recipe For the directions please refer to the chapter where I am talking about my 5 Minute 6 Step Juicing System.

Here is a short instruction that sums up what to do. Make sure to refer back to my 6 step process for juicing so that you get the whole idea of juicing.

In this case peel the cucumbers, apples and ginger.

Next cut and chop the fruits and veggies.

Put all the fruits and veggies from the ingredients list into your favorite juicer or blender or a combination of juicer/blender (Nutribullet) and strictly follow the directions of the manual that comes with your machine.

The manual will tell you what buttons to puch and what speed to use.

Juice the softer fruits/textures first.

You will see that when you are juicing the crunchier veggies and fruits they will help you push the softer and more delicate fruits and veggies through the blades.

Juice and Blend all the ingredients from the list above together as per instructions.

You can always add some raw honey or sweatener depending on your goal with these juices. If the juice is too strong for you, you might also add some ice cubes or source water.

Enjoy this Immune Booster!

Scrumptious Berry Juice

Ingredients:
  2 cups of fresh or frozen organic strawberries
  2 cups of fresh or frozen organic blueberries
  1.5 cups of fresh or frozen raspberries

Directions:

For the directions please refer to the chapter where I am talking about my 5 Minute 6 Step Juicing System.

Here is a short instruction that sums up what to do. Make sure to refer back to my 6 step process for juicing so that you get the whole idea of juicing.

Next cut and chop up all the fruits.

Put all the fruits from the ingredients list into your favorite juicer or blender or a combination of juicer/blender (Nutribullet) and strictly follow the directions of the manual that comes with your machine.

The manual will tell you what buttons to puch and what speed to use.

Juice and Blend all the ingredients from the list above together as per instructions.

Enjoy this empowering Scrumptious Berry Juice!

Remember, berries contain a rich source of antioxidants such as flavonoid, anthocyanins and ellagic acid and all of these antioxidants have a very good anti heart disease and anti cancer disease benefit.

Green & Red Super Energizer

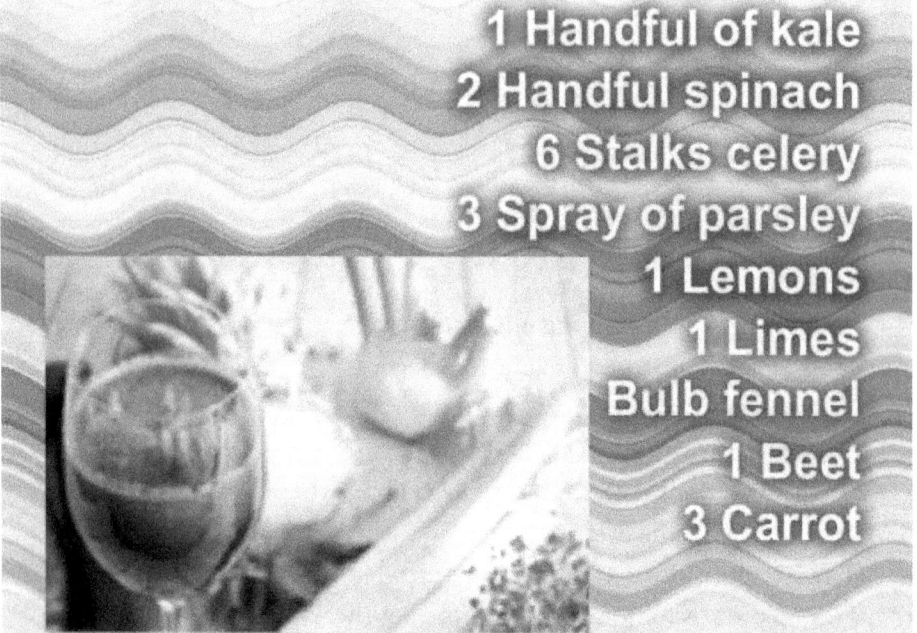

1 Handful of kale
2 Handful spinach
6 Stalks celery
3 Spray of parsley
1 Lemons
1 Limes
Bulb fennel
1 Beet
3 Carrot

The ingredients of the Red Kale Juice are all very beneficial for the body and brain.

The secret combination lies in the mix of red and green ingredients.

The beetroot is one of the most healthy vegetables on earth. Consuming beets will help you feel energized. Beets are great for nourishing your brain. It can assist in lowering blood pressure.

Beets contain a very broad amount of minerals and vitamins. Add some beets to your juices to instantly up and power pack your nutrients without adding more calories or fat. It contains folate and this helps prevnet cancer and heart diseases and Magnesium is keeping your energy levels up. It is also a very rich source of Vitamin C.

The alkaline Kale combined with the beets makes an unbeatable juice cocktail that helps you reenergize and rejuvenate at the same time. I enjoy one of these whenever my energy levels are down.

The Red Kale Juice contains the following ingredients:

Ingredients:

1 handful of kale (organic if possible)
2 handful spinach (organic if possible)
6 stalks of celery (organic if possible)
3 spray of parsley (organic if possible)
1 lemon (organic if possible)
1 lime (organic if possible)
½ bulb of fennel (organic if possible)
1 beet (organic if possible)
3 carrots (organic if possible)

Directions:

For all these juice recipe For the directions please refer to the chapter where I am talking about my 5 Minute 6 Step Juicing System.

Here is a short instruction that sums up what to do. Make sure to refer back to my 6 step process for juicing so that you get the whole idea of juicing.

In this case peel the lemons, limes, carrots, and beet (or buy prepared).

Next cut and chop the fruits and veggies.

Put all the fruits and veggies from the ingredients list into your favorite juicer or blender or a combination of juicer/blender (Nutribullet) and strictly follow the directions of the manual that comes with your machine.

The manual will tell you what buttons to puch and what speed to use.

Juice the softer fruits/textures first.

You will see that when you are juicing the crunchier veggies and fruits they will help you push the softer and more delicate fruits and veggies through the blades.

If you are not using a juicer and only have a blender available, make sure to first strain the juice from the lemon and lime.

Once it is finished you can either leave the pulp inside or take it out. This is totally up to your preference.

In this case you have to add the juice back to the blender and proceed from there.

Juice and Blend the juices with the other ingredients from the list above together as per instructions.

You can always add some raw honey or sweatener depending on your goal with these juices. If the juice is too strong for you, you might also add some ice cubes or source water.

Enjoy your Red Kale Juice!

Juicing For Doubling Your Life

Juicing truly benefits the body and the brain because it provides a combination of the most essential minerals, vitamins, amino acids, enzymes and essential fatty acids.

These veggies and fruits that are used in the juicing process are power packed with anti aging agents as well as life preserving elements.

The antioxidants and substances that neutralize the free radicals in the system ideally provide the possibility of having good anti aging benefits.

A juicing lifestyle filled with minerals and vitamins is the key factors. Juicing will also provide you with the benefit from antioxidants and substances that neutralize the free radicals which help the body fight against the aging process.

Make sure to include bright colored fruits as well as veggies into your daily juicing program because they are especially beneficial for the anti aging process. Make sure to pick fruits like cherries, oranges, tangerines, blueberries, apples, cranberries, bananas melons, grapes, kiwi, all red berries and mango because they are all very well know for their powerful anti aging properties.

These fruits and veggies can be taken separately or in combination with each other and depending on your taste.

When it comes to veggies make sure to include squash, carrots, green and red cabbages, spinach and broccoli because all of them are beneficial when it comes to the powerful anti aging properties.

Here are two juicing elexirs that help you stay young and double your life:

1. Orange Apple Detox

Ingredients:
1 fresh organic apple
1 slice of organic ginger root
1 organic carrot
½ cup of source water
Wash, peel, cut up, and juice as usual.

This juice contains excellent properties. You will grow healthy skin and you will eliminate nasty toxin form your system which is why this juice is so effective

2. Cholesterol Burning Empowerer
Ingredients:
1 fresh organic apple
½ fresh organic cucumber
4 stalks of organic celery
½ cup of source water
Wash, peel, cut up, and juice as usual.

This healthy and joung making elexir controls your high cholesterol levels. It also helps fight against an upset stomach. It is a true beautifier and you should be drinking it on a regular basis if your goal is to stay fit, sexy, healthy and young for a very long time.

The 5 Minute 9 Step Juicing Process

For all these juicing recipe simply follow my 5 minute step by step instructions.

First

Wash all veggies and fruits. Going through this thorough cleaning process will help prevent a nasty food-borne disease. I love to use organic vinegar because it is the most natural and organic solution, buy there are other options available if you prefer using products that are specifically designed for washing vegetables and fruits.

Second

Peel and cut all your fruits and veggies. Remember, you are juicing raw vegetables. This is why you need to cut them into small pieces before you get started. Especially if you are applying crunchier fruits and veggies such as carrots. Some high speed or high power juicers or a combination of juicer/blender like the Vitamix are able to take veggies and fruits in their whole form. In this case just follow the manufacturer's manual. Peel the skin of all your veggies and fruits. You also need to peel fruits like apples, melons, bananas, papaya, mango, pineapple, kiwis, banans, avocados, etc.

Next cut and chop the fruits and veggies such as leafy greens and fruits.

Third

Put your fruits and veggies into your favorite juicer or blender or a combination of juicer/blender (Nutribullet) and strictly follow the directions of the manual that comes with your machine. The manual will tell you what buttons to puch and what speed to use.

Juice the softer fruits/textures first.

You will see that when you are juicing the crunchier veggies and fruits they will help you push the softer and more delicate fruits and veggies through the blades.

If you are not using a juicer and only have a blender available, make sure to first strain the juice from citrus fruits like oranges, lemons, grapefruit, etc. When you are finished you can either leave the pulp inside the juice or take it out. It is totally up to your preference.

Next add the juice back to your mixture in the blender and proceed from there.

Fourth

Make sure to juice and blend everything together. Get the instructions from the manual that come with your juicer.

Raw honey is great so add it or use sweetener. It all depends on your own goal with juicing.

If your juicer is too strong for you, add some ice cubes or source water to your juice.

Usually, I only add ice cubes and source water to my smoothies, but some of my clients told me that they like to water down their juices. Some juices might just be a little bit too strong. This depends on the ingredients that you are using and your juicer and adding some water or ice cubes is the solution.

You will see that experimenting with juicing will help you discover many different varieties and alternatives that you can use.

Experimenting with juices is where the real fund begins so learn the basics first and the get creative.

Fivth

Try a variety of fruit and vegetable mixtures. As you experiment with juicing, you will find many combinations that you will enjoy on a daily basis. Some that pair well include apples with carrots, and leafy greens with kiwi. Try anything you want to taste. Create several go to recipes for yourself that you can use to make a healthy habit out of juicing.

Sixth

The last step is a very important one if you want to enjoy your juicer/blender for a very long time.

Make sure to clean your machine ASAP and once you are done with your juice.

This helps prevent nasty bacteria growth and in order to prevent any diseases that related to hygiene.

Use warm water and dish soap. You can also use vinegar to clean and then run the pieces through the dishwasher.

If you do not have a dishwahser take extra care with the cleaning process.

Seventh

Make sure to add lots of fiber to your smoothies, eat whole fruits and veggies throughout the day in order to stay balanced otherwise you might risk a dietary deficiency.

Eighth

Enjoy your refreshing and delicious juice and get you day started with lots of vitality and energy...

Nineth

Refer to chapter Juicing For Vitality & Energy to learn some more intriguing aspects that you can apply to your juicing lifestyle! The goal here is to keep the doctor away and reduce medical bills to ZERO cost and to double your life! (real money and time savers!)

Juicing Exexirs For Dropping The Pounds

Incorporating my morning juice elexir plus keeping a daily juicing and smoothie ritual into a pound dropping weight loss diet plan is a very effective way to get these pound dropping results.

Always make sure to include a mixture of both veggies and fruits. Focusing only on the sweet fruits will not be as beneficial as applying a combination of both because most fruits usually have a high contents of sugar.

If your goal is to drop pounds with juicing here are some very effective ways to do just that:

Green veggies and pineapple: This concoction is bursting with goodness for the body. It is simply a refreshing juice plus you get the advantage that you feels satisfied and not hungry

Apple and berry fiber: The apples help because they are an excellent cleansing agent. The berries, on the other hand, provide you with the mineral supplements that you need during a diet.

Oranges and pineapple: Both a rich sourche of vitamin C. This elexir provides you with enzymes that can dissolve mucus accumulated in your body. It also helps speed up your metabolism which helps dropping the pounds.

Ginger and pear: This is a great concoction and a laxative option. This juice is a very good option if you are looking for a good digestion which in the end provides you with a very natural and healthy pound dropping solution.

Effortless Juicing Process To Maximize Your Pound Dropping Results

Preserve yourself from overeating by drinking a big cup of juices well before eating.

If you are able to pinpoint a juice extractor that is certainly high quality and operates on lower speeds, this would be your best choice. Increased speed might overheat your machine and thus destroy the nutrients of your juices.

Make sure to refer to the Green Star Juicer Review which has advantages as opposed to other juicers in relation to this overheating issue.

If you are in an age bracket over 50, you should be thinking to include juicing into your lifestyle in order to reduce the process of aging.

Pick a product or service which can be premium quality, simple to use and valued to match within your spending budget.

Add ginger to your juices and meal plan. Adding ginger to your juices also provides you with zesty flavor. Ginger also has a anti inflammatory quality. It helps you recover injuries.

Purchase a masticating juice extractor which will keep the nutrition in the juices that you are making.

If you prefer juices without the pulp, I recommend to use an espresso filtration system or some cheesecloth to filter out the pulp.

Make sure to always include green super foods like kale, broccoli and spinach into your juices and shoot for 50%-75% plant based ingredients plus some other veggies and fruits for the sweet flavoring and to balance the sometimes bitter flavor of the veggies.

Should you be juicing as a result of health problems, make sure to get started with dark green fruits and leafy vegetables as your basic juices.

Never use industrial fruit juices to replace real fruits because they are full of natural sweets and consist of much less nutrients and vitamins than fresh juices.

If you do not like the bitter taste of some veggies make sure to balace the flavor with fruits like apples. In my opinion apples like Fuji, Rome, and Gala are the providing the best flavour.

When attempting to lose weight with juicing, try to create pineapple liquid with your juicer and you will find that adding apples are a wonderful combination with pineapple juice.

If you are on a juicing diet, you may want to lower the calories by adding an equal amount of ice cubes or source water.

Make time for yourself to truly enjoy your juices and try to get a feel for the different ingredients and flavors.

Juicing is even much easier and much more fun when the entire family takes part in the process. Have a child wash the fruits and veggies while a grown-up chops and processes it. If you include your kids, you will keep them interested and integrated into a healthy lifestyle at an early age which will benefit the health of your child enormously. Imagine not having to run to the doctor for every disease the child might come up with!

Make sure to respect the amounts and the combination with real healthy food because juicing alone is not a solution. It is always meant in a way to substitute your healthy daily diet in order to keep you and your family fit based on the highly nutritious value that you will be supplied with from these healthy juices.

Make sure to research and know the benefits of the veggies and fruits that you are using. Every single vegetable and fruit gives distinct vitamins and nutrients and you must be aware what they do for you.

Improve your every day intake of nutrients by making juicing part of your eating habits. Your whole body will reap the benefits plus you will find that these juices are not only healthy and fat burning in nature, but these juices are also super easy to make and taste deliciously.

Juicing is a simple to acquire skill and if you turn this skill into a habit, you will be able to live a clean, toxin free and lean life from the inside out and for a very long time.

Juicing keeps the doctor away and doubles your life!

The Juice Fasting Weight Loss Factor

Juicing removes fiber from nutrient dense food. Make sure to include an appropriate amount of fiber rich food in your daily diet plan. Juicing should be a complement to a well balanced healthy diet, not a complete substitute.

Make sure to eat whole fruits and veggies or drink smoothies with fiber because juicing has the tendency to remove fiber which is an important nutrient. Fiber helps keep the digestion on a balanced level and fiber keeps your cholesterol in control.

Make sure to add lots of fiber to your smoothies, eat whole fruits and veggies throughout the day in order to stay balanced otherwise you might risk a dietary deficiency.

You will find that your appetite finds raw foods more filling. Cooking foods can cause the loss of up to 97 percent of water soluble vitamins A, E, D and K.

Uncooked and raw foods such as juices do contain more vitamins and nutrients. These nutrients are more satisfying to the body which means that the body's metabolism will keep running efficiently. Consuming these juices will keep your weight loss efforts focused and you are going into the right direction.

Juicing also helps kick start the digestive process of the body and enables a very quick absorption of high quality nutrition which leads to an increased energy level of your body.

If weight loss is your ultimate goal with juicing then you must understand that by applying juicing as a weight loss solution is a very natural way of losing weight.

You must understand the fact that achieving weight loss through improved nutrition like juicing is one of the best benefits of juicing and if weight loss is your goal this fact alone should be very motivational for you. Take advantage of this side effect of juicing. I call this the effortless way of losing weight as opposed to going through some weird and complicated diets that are replacing some bad things that you should not eat anymore. Usually the latest and greatest fad diets tell you to replace the bad stuff with the good stuff but in a very unnatural and extreme way.

A diet in general does not work because it is too demanding, unrealistic and too extreme. I never succeeded in losing weight by following a diet because in the end I gained all the weight that I lost in a very unnatural and suppressing way. Juicing is the only natural way that I know of that gives the body all nutrients that it needs while still being able to lose weight because the weight loss kind of happens as a natural side effect and automatically.

Remember that juicing does remove the fiber so be sure to always include fiber rich food in your daily diet plan that you are following with your juicing for weight loss goals.

In my case, when I lost 40 lbs with juicing and smoothies I did not follow an extreme diet that in my opinion is just a waste of time.

I followed my daily juicing and smoothie riutal and followed a light and healthy fiber rich meal plan without following a particular complicated diet plan that some genius health guru figured out. I had lots of fibers, vegetables, protein like lean chicken and avoided food with fat and sugar. Instead of white bread, I opted for whole wheat, etc. without following any complicated diet plans or formulas that keep tricking the body into believing something that in the end leads to some catastrophic disaster. I consumed just natural, organic and lean food without fat and sugar in order to get enough fiber because the juices do not provide enough fiber.

If you are using juicing to lose weight, you really must understand that juicing should only be a complement to a well balanced healthy and natural diet, not a substitute because this would again make it an unnatural and extreme process which is why most diets do not work!

As you can see juicing is a very natural process and the opposite of an extreme diet. If you follow these rules, you will soon discover that your body learns to function in a very effective and balanced way that helps you lose weight and keep your weight off effectively while keeping you satisfied;

Once you have achieved a metabolism that balances itself naturally while losing weight in the process and while being able to keep the weight off, you will understand the difference between a lifestyle with juicing which is a very natural process and a diet. By following a diet you have to respect some weird and complicated plan. With juicing you are living a lifestyle that I can call a happy, healthy, natural, balanced, satisfied, clean and lean eating lifestyle.

So as you can see with a little planning and creativity, the process of juicing can enhance your well being, health and your well balanced diet which in turn helps you lose weight in an automatic and very natural way.

All the recipes that I have included in this juicing book are great for getting started with juicing for weight loss. These recipes helped me lose 40 lbs in 2 months and many of my family members and friends that have tried them out achieved similar results.

Go through them as you see fit and apply my tips for juicing for weight loss and you will find a great satisfaction and balance once you are done.

You will discover for yourself that juicing is very beneficial and that you want to keep the habit of juicing. This is how you will be able to live a lifestyle free of diseases and toxins. This is how you keep your body lean and clean. This is how you keep the doctor away. This is how you stay beautiful, keep balance, stay healthy and fit from the inside out and this is how you ultimately double your life!

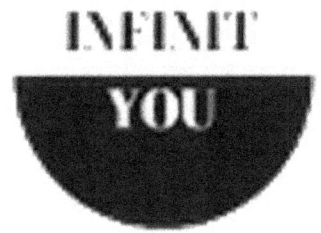

About the Publisher

InfinitYou is a hybrid general interest trade publisher. One of the first of its kind InfinitYou publishes physical books, electronic books, and audiobooks in various genres. Our publications are meant to educate, edify and entertain readers of all walks of life from babies to the elderly. Home to more than twenty imprints such as Infinit Baby, Infinit Kids, Infinit Girl, Infinit Boy, Infinit Coloring, Infinit Swear Words, Infinit Activities, Infinit Productivity, Infinit Cat, Infinit Dog, Infinit Love, Infinit Family, Infinit Survival, Infinit Health, Infinit Beauty, Infinit Spirituality, Infinit Lifestyle, Infinit Wealth, Infinit Romance, and lots more.

www.ingramcontent.com/pod-product-compliance
Lightning Source LLC
LaVergne TN
LVHW012106070526
838202LV00056B/5647